WOW!!!

WINDOWS OF WISDOM

TERRY E. LYLE

Order this book online at www.trafford.com
or email orders@trafford.com

Most Trafford titles are also available at major online book retailers.

Edited by Tracy Duke Arnold.
Trafford publishers.
Photography by Terryatte E. Lyle.

Note for Librarians: A cataloguing record for this book is available from Library and Archives Canada at www.collectionscanada.ca/amicus/index-e.html

Printed in the United States of America.

ISBN: 978-1-4269-1337-2 (sc)
ISBN: 978-1-4269-1338-9 (dj)

Library of Congress Control Number: 2009931989

Our mission is to efficiently provide the world's finest, most comprehensive book publishing service, enabling every author to experience success. To find out how to publish your book, your way, and have it available worldwide, visit us online at www.trafford.com/10510

Trafford rev. 8/7/2009

 www.trafford.com

North America & international
toll-free: 1 888 232 4444 (USA & Canada)
phone: 250 383 6864 ♦ fax: 250 383 6804

About the Authoress

Terry Lyle is an award winning authoress, whose first work, a book of poetry entitled "Brown Bag Poetry" via Trafford Publishers, is still making heads turn since its release in December of 2008. Now she's back with her newly released book entitled "WOW"!!!

For the individuals who know Terry up close and personal, they will tell you that she's a keeper. She is a very energetic, funny, upbeat, and laugh a minute type person. Terry is compassionate and family oriented. She has a real soft spot for children, church, and people in need. Terry is very loyal and long suffering with her friends; however, she is firm but fair in her beliefs, as she hides her shyness when thrust into a group of people who are waiting to hear her speak.

Terry is very intelligent, extremely honest, and often lacks the subtlety of adhering to your ego. Terry, while brutally raw and in your face with the truth, believes that we all need a reality check from time to time. While big on integrity, she always states, "Integrity is free, so live like it and stand for truth." She realizes everyone can change, so she doesn't judge you on your past mistakes, but she will observe your present actions. Trust and respect is a requirement if close bonds with her are possible. Terry contributes her kind spirit to the glory of God and her strict, yet nurturing upbringing. Terry's spiritual growth soared when she became a member of the Huber Memorial Church in Baltimore, Maryland under the guidance of Pastor P.M. Smith and after being added to the South Girard Church of Christ in Phenix City, Alabama under the guidance of Minister Samuel Alexander.

Terry is truly a blessing to have and know as a friend and family member. If you cross paths with her then, I'm sure you will agree that she will leave impressions of her footprints in your heart, and a smile on your face as you stroll down memory lane. This refreshing change is depicted as well in her writing style and your words of choice I'm sure will be, "WOW"!!!

Respectfully submitted by her brother, Phillip Robertson

Dedication

I dedicate this book to everyone who dares
to dream. When things seem hopeless, remain hopeful, and stay encouraged. Through
Christ, all things are possible. I also dedicate this book globally to the Churches of
Christ, with special mention of South Girard
Church of Christ in Phenix City, Alabama,
with Minister Samuel Alexander presiding.

Acknowledgements

*Along the pathway of life you meet a
few people who leave footprints on your
heart that never should be forgotten!!!*

These are the individuals who, in my darkest moments, or difficult times, came through for me in a big way by their supportive, physical, and monetary manner and never gave up on me. They are as follows:

Auntie Carol Lucille Robertson, and Aunt Sarah Murphy, Kumar, Olu, Stan & Cynthia Snead, Michael Gaigler, Manya A.Washington, Deborah Baldwin, James Josey, Tracy Arnold, La Cori Patrice Arnold, Isaiah Arnold, Harold & Jason Scott, Pastor P.M. Smith & Delores Stanton-Smith, Alfansa Robinson, Thomas Robinson, Louie Anderson, Lloyd Carter, Pastor Sylvestor & Mrs. Willow Feagins, Louise Childs, Dr. Xavier McCaskey, Larry & Sarah Chambers, Carl Reeder, Mrs. June Coleman, Joanne Bland, Dr. Rita Harvey, Mr. & Mrs. Henry & Zara Parham, Reginald Massengill, Ariana Irene Brown, and my beautiful cousins Barbara Fleming White, Veronica A. Odum, William C. Robinson (Little Bill), Tyrone Anderson, and Rodney Murphy.

For those of you whom I have overlooked, if I know you by face and name, you have also left an impression. But the people listed above deserve credit for coming through when no one else did. Their show of love became an action word, which left me speechless most of the time when all I could think was "WOW"!!!

WOW!!!

Welcome

to

#

This is a collection of short stories which speaks the truth about a vast array of situations that will have you hungry for more at its conclusion.

Enjoy your reading and share with your family and friends; they will be glad that you did.

Terry E. Lyle

Tables of Contents

WOW!!!

Terry E. Lyle

WOW!!!

Terry E. Lyle

WOW!!!

Terry E. Lyle

This Book entitled WOW!!!

This book is totally clean and legit, it's wonderfully awesome and it does the trick. The thoughts are powerful and on the mark, as you're definitely delighted right from the start.

Now WOW, it's my second work, and it's so good you can take it to church. Now people had some remarks about book number one, but trust and believe I got the job done.

Now Brown Bag Poetry was book number one, it included some racy stuff, which made you run. Now run fast, and quickly you did, just to tell someone else about what you just read.

I just want you to know that I'm here to stay; Terry Lyle is going to bring it your way. Up close and personal I will be in your grill, while your story, I'm going to reveal.

I'm going to reveal some truths that need to be told, while making it plain that is my goal. People generally experience the very same things, but I'm going to put you on Front Street, while keeping it clean.

I will expose the issues and bring them out front, while I speak for you and deliver the punch. This is my talent and that is true, because I can roll with the punches and deliver some too.

So I won't be afraid to speak what's on your mind, I'll be the villain and you can be kind. Some people you have to nail to the cross, they act like peacocks and strut like your boss.

But I am here to avenge the soul, because I will tell the stories that need to be told. Never will I back down from strife, give me a good challenge and I'm up for the fight. So here comes the one, two, POW!!! Enjoy this book that's entitled "WOW"!!!

Terry E. Lyle

Brown Bag Poetry

I wrote a poem, like you have asked me to do. I'm still trying to tweak it until I get back to you. Call me back later I'll be here waiting on you, still writing my poetry is the thing that I do. If I wanted to sell something that's truly a part of me, then let it be my first book titled "Brown Bag Poetry". While patiently I wait for those benefits I'll see, I'll continue writing most diligently. It was a long time ago when I was told, "Terry, use your skills before your raggedy butt gets old, you should try writing children's books, because you'd be good at that," but stupid old me still haven't done it yet. I should go ahead, do it, and get some things in motion; take a vacation, while I cruise on the ocean. I can start making some money while gaining some respect; if I get my ducks in a row then I will be set. Making some money has always been my dream, other than flying or being a queen. I have done some dumb things and I do them a lot, my mom would be screaming that it's time that I stop! My friends are tripping from the things that I say, especially Louise Childs on any given day. As a matter of fact here's what she would say, "Terry don't start with me, please not today, you're full of crap and I don't want to play". Sometimes in your life you don't know who you should trust, people will stir up some emotions that will bring you to cuss. Slithering around trying to steal your joy and acting friendly is their sick little ploy. They want to gain your confidence before they go on attack, but keep turning around while you cover your back. They can do what they want and say what they will, because "Brown Bag Poetry" is a dream that's already fulfilled. Now WOW!!! Is my current book that you're reading right now, it's a hidden treasure that you've just found?

The Truth

The truth is the truth, it doesn't change over time. People often dance around the truth. Reality of the truth initially appears painful, but strengthens you as time goes by. The truth is often concealed, but felt inwards. You curse truth when it shows up unexpectedly. The truth will make you cry and humble yourself. The truth will point its finger at you. The truth is usually accompanied by white lies, often they bicker about their position. The truth is the undefeated contender, and always the champion. The truth is timeless, yet people try to ignore or abandon her. The truth is fearless, you may not want to acknowledge her, but she'll make you take a hard look at yourself. The truth is the foundation of love, and often persecuted. However, the truth is the truth.

Terry E. Lyle

God's Whisper

Do you listen to your reservations? Maybe it's intuition or God's whisper. Remember the times when you were in situations that you shouldn't have been? Or at a place where you stayed too long? Your pulse raced, and your mind was agitated and you had that nagging, insistent desire to change your plans. You wondered, "Is this God's whisper? You constantly second guess your choices, afraid to trust that voice inside of you. No, I'm not perfect, only Christ is. People in their imperfections should try to compromise and work at interacting with others so that they don't appear so abrasive. Have you ever thought that when you're on the wrong path, maybe that nagging feeling to stop or change your ways is God's whisper? How do you listen? Is it with a compassionate heart or is it with your ears that you hear God's whisper?

Boycotted

I think that I've been boycotted because of the looks on their face. Some turn away and hide their disgrace. People won't even talk to me as I come in the room; I don't understand why over me this dark cloud still looms. All I did was to write a book, where I talked about life and the chances people took. Some poems were graphic, and some were clean, but I was only trying to be honest and I wasn't trying to be mean.

I must admit however that some people really loved my work, they read the book from cover to cover, and left fingerprint dirt. Some were really shocked at the things I had to say, but in reality those things happen each and every day. Some people love to be secretive, and act like goody two shoes; however I've busted that bubble, because the things I have talked about you know you can relate to.

People are now whispering all behind my back and if their eyes could shoot me, I would be under attack. One thing I don't understand is, if you ever liked me then why the big demands. Let me write my book the way that I can. Disappointing you is not what I'm trying to do, I'm just trying to give you reading pleasure while you relax and kick off your shoes.

So some people have decided to boycott me, I'm not mad because they can do as they please. It's really their choice to do, because what you think only concerns you. I'll keep writing my stuff and saying what's true, and you can join them on your soapbox too. If being boycotted is what it has to be, then "Oh well then do as you please".

Terry E. Lyle

My Life

My heart is sympathetic towards you. If I'm not helping you, then you're not respecting me, so I think, "Why am I wasting my time?" I feel stupid sometimes because I don't listen to my heart; after all, this is my life. I know that I shouldn't talk to you, but I find myself drawn towards you. You have a habit of saying that I'm sensitive and maybe I am in some things; however, I realize I will no longer tolerate you getting angry at me about what you think that I'm thinking. How ludicrous is this? You're angry about your own perceptions. Immediately your thoughts are negative and sarcastic when you're hurt, corrected, or embarrassed about your own insensitivity. You shield yourself in an attempt to not face your realities. How often do I shield you from the unpleasantness and pain of humility? You are your own worst critic and I am your biggest fan; and yet, you steal the cheer right out of my heart. You allow paranoia and negativity to infest your brain in an insidious manner, all because you have forgotten how to love yourself. I choose to allow you into to my life. How long should I allow you to dwell there? If I don't talk to you, then I can get over you. The bottom line is that I have to live my life for myself, regardless of what others think of me. Since I've reached the age of maturity, I'm entitled to do as I please without reservations. If my actions don't physically affect anyone else, my choices shouldn't be dictated as well. Every day I have to defend myself with you. I'm not a punk though, so do what you do, and I'll do what I must. After all, this is my life.

WOW!!!

Swollen Feet

My feet are swollen very badly and they look like they will pop. I walk real gently on them while I constantly say ouch. I take my meds for my pressure, but it really doesn't help at all. When all I do is piss my brains, while I'm climbing up the wall. I can't sit very long, it really tears me up. My feet and legs get real big and that's the part that sucks. I know I have medical problems; tell me who doesn't have them too. If you tell me you don't know anyone, I'll say that you're a fool. I'm really talking about the ones who have reached 40 and above. It seems like that's when all hell breaks loose for no reason; just because. The cost of prescriptions these days will make your wallets burst. It's real easy to see how things have really gotten worst. So as I struggle with my feet, and do what I must do. I hope today and pray please don't swell... but fit inside my shoes!!!

Terry E. Lyle

Disabled

Disabled is what I don't want to be, unfortunately, that is what I see. My body doesn't work the way it used to. It aches real badly and I can't even tie my shoes. Bending over has become a chore, the pain is intense and I can't take anymore. I'm popping pills each and every day in hopes that my pain will soon go away. Little things I used to do are helpful things, now done by you. People are helpful as they see your struggles, even on a plane they help you buckle. Wheelchair clients they will go on first, because we all realize, their pain is the worst. No longer take for granted, the good health that you have, unless you enjoy sitting on your ass. Think how hard it is to clean yourself, when you need the help of someone else! You sit in a chair trying to fix your meals; because you can't afford to have anything spill. Laundry day is truly a drag; having to sort clothes in two different bags. Bending over is hard on the back, the slightest move and it's gone out of whack. Now let me tell you about the knees; they will swell and ache and you can't walk with ease. When your eyes start to mess up and you don't see too well, you will squint, like there's something bad that you smell. If any part of the body isn't feeling too good, and the things you wanted to do you wish that you could, that's a sign that you have been labeled, and unfortunately the term is called disabled.

I can't wrap my mind around that

Didn't you tell me that you were staying in the house all day, saying you wanted to relax? I'm tired of leaving a message and you won't answer the phone, where are you because you should be at home? I can't wrap my mind around that.

Didn't you tell me that you were in pain, and that you needed a nap? Fifteen minutes later you lifting things too heavy for your back, but I can't wrap my mind around that.

Didn't you tell me that I talk too loud? But you're the one heard in a really noisy crowd, and I can't wrap my mind around that.

Didn't you tell me to be ready to go to a movie tonight? Because you don't want to be late, and you don't want to fight, but when I get to your house on you I have to wait. Time is ticking and it's getting really late, but I can't wrap my mind around that.

Didn't you tell me I needed to stop eating so many sweets, but your mouth is bulging with candy that you constantly eat? Well I decided to write a book, plus I really hate to read even though my work is marvelous, yes marvelous indeed. So go figure, "How should I wrap my mind around that"?

Hollow words

Irritation just below the surface, because my face cracks with disgust and your words are hollow. You think as long as you have an excuse the world is supposed to swallow your empty promises and suck it up without an explanation or apology. My time doesn't mean a thing as long as your excuses make sense to you. But I see that you're hollow, lack follow-through, and are rather insensitive to people's feelings when they differ from yours. Yet I'm supposed to understand you, but you're hollow.

You find yourself angered at being questioned about your movements, because you lack an acceptable time table to follow through on plans made. Inside your mind I would never begin to imagine how it works, I'm afraid I would fall through the cracks of your limitations, and become swallowed whole by the seeds of discontentment in your mind.

You run to and fro to the needs of everyone else, except me, to seek their admiration and acceptance, while your close friends are standing on the outside looking in. I find myself battling for your time and attention, while I dust off the pedestal that I've placed you on, knowing my victory was hollow in concept to begin with.

Warmth has turned into ugliness, because my feelings you treat with such disregard. Carelessly you expect me to wait quietly until you squeeze me into your schedule, and your affection appears hollow, like your words.

WOW!!!

I was just thinking

I was just thinking about the different people in my life and how they affect it. Some have a positive effect and others tend to slowly damage the better qualities that I possess. Have you ever wondered why when someone violates your trust and respect that, they get mad at you because you don't accept their apologies? Yet they messed up and they want you to get over it. How do you begin the cycle of trust? I can't do it. I find myself sickened to my core when someone I believed in and trusted hurts me with callous disregard. I try to imagine what they may be feeling and all I come up with is attention seekers, who thrive on dishonesty to validate their ineffectiveness. Some would surmise that maybe I should feel sorry for them, but I can't find a single reason to justify the lie in someone you care for, especially if it shatters your world. Have you thought about me? Apparently not...so I suck it up and move on, leaving behind sweet memories of support and loyalty. Thank God for the few people who stand behind their words and actions. In them is integrity and trust; the soldiers of humanity, who seek to encourage and uplift at personal loss. Yet no one hears their cries, while in their misery they vow to not get too close again, because the damages are mounting. But you never know! I was just thinking....

Parenthood

Parenthood is not about reciprocation it is about obligation. When you bring life into the world, you need to assist them through the age of maturity so that you can set them free. Hopefully the wisdom you have given them will shelter them along the path to adulthood. There they can reach back and teach their children pearls of wisdom that has been instilled in them through your guidance. There will be many different roads to take and many hard choices to make. Once leaving from the starting gate, let love be your inspiration, while on their growth you wait.

Disrespected

What is it like to be disrespected is a question that have different meanings, yet the underlined truth is that it's always painful. Disrespect is inflicted upon you by someone out of control and rather childish. After looking past the horrible words and actions, you will see a person full of self doubt and low self esteem. Mature adults know how to harness their tongue from idiotic defamatory remarks that usually describes the ignoramus using them. The victims of disrespect are internally bruised by harsh words and actions. The brain tries to digest what happened and why, and the body speaks out through tears of humiliation, and the ears burn with anger and thoughts of retaliation. True strength is seen when a victim of disrespect can boldly hold back from the verbal tit for tat without attacking or damaging the ego of the speaker. To be ridiculed while maintaining integrity shows honor and respectable qualities, that a fool couldn't understand. A fool glories in their own little mindset that's too narrow to grasp common sense, yet loud and boisterous they grandstand to solicit attention and laughs. Not realizing that they also disrespected themselves by setting the morality bar so low. Basically one thing should be remembered, and that is…to get respect you need to give respect.

Terry E. Lyle

Negro Please!!!

It's eleven forty-five p.m. at night and I'm just hanging out doing my thing. I am very relaxed and comfortable. My brassiere is off and my toes are free. Suddenly I hear knocking on my door which made me jump up to scramble for clothes, so I could arrange myself and see who had the gall to be at my door at this time of night. As I yelled through the door, I heard a familiar voice respond back to me. Quickly I decided to let this Negro in...so I could put him in check face to face. Smiling sweetly I asked him to sit down. While pissed I go in for the kill, "why are you here at this time of night and why didn't you call first?" Talk about some fancy footwork around the truth, this man had the audacity to imply he thought about me and came over strictly to hang out with me, Negro please!!! Tell me, what can we do this time of night and where would we go that's open on a midweek night? How dare you assume that you were going to get your happy butt into my bed, to dump your liquids into me? Especially coming up in here empty handed.... Negro, please!!! If I were a whore or some hood rat, you had better bet it, you would be shelling out some money at the minimum! Yet still you want to smell my fresh supple body and run your greedy hands all over me, but won't pay for the supplies. What about the perfumes, soaps, and the douches that I have to pay for? What about the light bill, rent or things that a real man will contribute towards without asking? If I wanted a wet derriere I could easily jump into the shower but you insist on bringing your nappy head behind over here, because you thought about me at eleven forty- five at night, Negro please!!!

WOW!!!

Listless

I'm awake, even though it doesn't feel special; I'm up never the less. I look like crap, my body hurts, and my breath isn't too fresh. I want to do something productive, but I feel listless. I tilt my head and my neck cracks, feels like I'm falling apart at the seams. My stomach is growling, and I'm hungry, I can't move because I feel listless. I look at myself and I look a hot mess, I don't care because I feel listless. I'm too lazy to even take my medicine, only thing I will do is use the toilet because I feel listless. I sit here and wonder what lie I can tell, so I can stay home, I'm not sick, I just feel listless. I don't even want to answer my phone; I'll just sit here and look stupid, because I feel listless. As I walk away while farting back to my bed, I decide to lie back down because I feel listless. Oh no someone is knocking on my door, I can't do this today I'll have to be quiet and pretend I'm not home, because I feel listless. I hate days like these where you feel crappy and crazy. I don't want to venture out because I feel listless. Or maybe not, I could just be lazy.

Terry E. Lyle

Uncomfortable

Uncomfortable feelings; I've had a few and if you're honest, then maybe you've had some too. I remember when I first wore heels, very unsteady until that very first spill. I went down on my butt with a very big thump; I landed real hard while bruising my rump. My feet twisted over, and down I went, people were laughing and my feelings were bent. I remember when I was on my menstrual cycle, and messed up my clothes. Blood showed through, now everyone knew. Oops I thought with an embarrassing glow. A lot of things have happened to me, that maybe I should quietly keep under wraps. I'm not trying to be vulgar; I'm just stating the facts. I remember the first time I lost my virginity. How painful it was and how stupid I felt. I didn't know what to do and I needed some help. I worried about whether I'll get pregnant, or catch a disease. I gave away my virginity because of his pleads. However he waited four years before he got it, because I had so many mixed feelings about it. Sex without marriage left me full of doubt, so I married this man because it was right. A baby followed relatively quick and new problems arrived lickety-split. I can't remember all the uncomfortable times that I've had, but when I felt them I was embarrassed and sad.

Old Age

I remember the days when my house was so full of fun. People coming and going, now those days are over and done. Now these days I serve meals only for a few, my constant guests are Father Time with Mother Nature too. I hide all the mirrors because I don't really want to see, that I'm not as pretty as I once used to be. I've put on some extra weight, and I have some chubby weak knees, things have gotten so bad for me that now I start to wheeze. The lines of maturity they show all over my face, multiple love handles are now piled around my waist. My hair has thinned out, and sometimes I even wear a wig, I need to have some way to hide and cover up my head. Pill bottles have accumulated from two now to eight. So many pills I unfortunately regularly have to take. Reading glasses they are a must and my attention span is short. I start so many projects that often I have to abort. But now I'm getting older and really don't care so much. Sometimes I'll be fussing, and cussing and don't know why I acted out as such. My mouth seems to be getting raggedy, my teeth they are falling out of my face, way in the back of my mouth you will find there is a lot of space. My breasts have gotten heavy, and no longer will they stand, having perky titties will have to be brought on my new insurance plan. My insurance coverage is paid up, and I'm still waiting here to die. I hope one day that I am missed, and make somebody cry. Let me leave a good memory, and I hope you know it's true. I lived my life fully and I always loved you too. So when you think of me, and people begin to talk, just remember and know this fact inside that "my bite wasn't as bad as my bark."

Terry E. Lyle

Don't go Grandma

I'm going to see my grandkids because I haven't seen them in awhile. I am going to see my grandkids because they always make me smile. I like to see those little faces, when they come running towards me. I'm hiding candy in my pockets which I know that they will see. They know their grandmother wants to pinch them, hug, kiss and squeeze, while wiping away their boo-boo's, and bandage the skinned up knees. Grandma loves them very much, and they are sorely missed, when grandma sits at home alone, and miss their special kiss. When it's time to go, they hug her and they sigh. Then they start to whimper, as she watches those babies cry. "Don't go grandma, don't go, please stay a little while, don't go grandma, and I promise we won't cry. Can you stay five minutes more, while I look into your eyes? We want to tell you something that comes from all of us, which are here; grandma I hate to tell you this, your wig is sliding off your head! Don't go grandma, don't go, and please don't be too mad because I had to tell you, your hair is looking bad."

WOW!!!

Growing Pains

When you try to introduce something new and unfamiliar into your life, that period of adjustment is considered growing pains.

When you see problems in a relationship as reasons to jump ship without a life preserver, this is considered nothing but growing pains.

Have you heard the expression, "Get in where you fit in"? These are little steps of growth. Doing and being a part of something, as you shape your personality, is considered growing pains.

Emotional ups and downs, stress factors, financial woes, and headaches are all considered growing pains.

From zero to ninety-nine years of age, from infancy to adulthood, from loved to loveless, and from start to finish, life is fueled with growing pains.

Terry E. Lyle

Stealing

It's a real thought for concern, when someone steals the things you've earned. They have violated that sacred trust, when doing what's right should have been a must. Stealing will get you in trouble; you could ruin your life and turn it to rubble.

When you take an item without permission, it's my strong conviction that your life lacks ambition. What would make you think that stealing is ok? How did your family raise you, may I ask anyway?

You don't have the right to steal my stuff. That's a horrible thing to do which leaves me miserable and want to fuss. You should have been raised better than that, so if you stole something then please return it and give it back.

I'm not trying to hear your excuses. What you did is considered ruthless. Just taking what you wanted to have, not considering whom it belonged to or even who had it last. You need to humble yourself and make some amends, so you won't be restricted from returning again.

You should leave a thing alone that doesn't belong to you; because stealing is a nasty habit you shouldn't want to do. Once you begin to steal, then people won't even trust you, and have thoughts on their mind on how to kill you.

WOW!!!

Quiet Times

What do you do in your quiet times? Sometimes I do nothing and just hang out on the bed, and reflect on my day.

Other times I play on my computer and surf the net. Maybe I'll make it a DVD night. Sometimes I read my bible, even thou not as often as I should.

Quiet times I wish sometime to share with someone special. Or quietly listen to the sounds of traffic as it goes by.

Sometimes in my quiet time, I lay and cry, not because of grief but for the awful release of pressures of my day.

After which I humble myself and kneel and pray.

Terry E. Lyle

Where's my mail?

I know my package was sent off in the mail, but where it went I don't know where. All I know is that it hasn't arrived in the mail; I'm so irritated that I will scream and I yell.

Now I'm chasing the mailman down, each and every time I see him come, with an expression on my face that really looks dumb. Trying to figure out in my mind how come the mail is so late, knowing all the time that I'm tired of this tedious long wait.

With thoughts on my mind that aren't very kind, seems like I hate the post office now most of the time. They haven't delivered my mail and I still wonder why, I'm especially mad and now I want to cry.

I'm playing phone tag each and every day, calling about my package that now is delayed. I'm really flustered as you probably can tell all because I haven't received my overdue mail.

Where is my mail can somebody please tell me, because this tedious wait is killing me, because I'm truly flustered indeed?

The path of the storm

The sky was dark blue, and approaching across the horizon were storm clouds. I wondered how bad was this going to be, will the storm pass over? Within minutes, a constant pounding against my window pane was thumping loudly as if an intruder was trying to get in.

Huddled beneath my blankets, I trembled as my lights began to flicker, with the loud emergency sirens blaring in the distance. How long would the storm last? How long would it devastate everything in its path?

A cold eerie silence came upon the room. Then in an instant, a flash of blinding lightning filled the room, followed by a crackling and rumbling of thunder. The hairs on my neck became prickly, because of my fear of the storm. All alone and frightened, I began to pray for sleep, so I could ride out the storm peacefully in my slumber.

I scrambled to find a sleeping pill because the tension intensified. I'm not sure of whether there will be extensive damage to my home or injuries to myself because I was caught in the path of the storm. Loud thunder rumbling and lightning illuminating the room in its scary brightness, as car horns were going off and strong gusty sounds of the wind blew outside, knocking things around against my home.

Terry E. Lyle

As I listened to the emergency sirens going off in the distance, I wondered why I didn't heed the evacuation warnings that were made all day long. I didn't listen and now I find myself stuck in the path of the storm. I thought I would be brave enough to stay so I could watch my possessions, which I now find underwater, as I scramble to the roof. I hope someone will be brave enough to venture out to find me, while I am stuck in the path of the storm.

Damaged People

I'm damaged and I'm sure you are as well, but we keep things a secret when your story you should tell. Wondering why you are always loving yourself less, when you should love yourself the very best.

We all have a past with things we would like to hide, dark ugly secrets we store deep inside. Abandonment, molestation and brutality to say the least, these are some of those ugly things that cause us such disgrace, but if you live long enough it'll get thrown in your face.

Young kids suffering and they have nowhere to turn, while not feeling happy when its love that they yearn. There are sick individuals snacking on innocence of youth, not being a role model but inflicting the abuse.

Young mothers having kids too soon, they grow up latch key children and left alone, at home, frightened in their rooms. Watching and waiting for their next warm meal. Some days they get none and sometimes grow ill.

Echoes of tears heard silently in my head, thinking about moments that I wish I were dead. I have misunderstanding about what really is love, when I should have known it came from above.

Terry E. Lyle

Even though these issues don't apply to me, I needed to verbalize this so everyone could see; it's an honor to be blessed with a child, so protect them the best way that you know how. Help our children grow into reasonable adults, who don't blame others for their own inbred type faults.

My message to you is there is damage in everyone, but you can rise from this and forget the damage that's done. You are very special and should love yourself first; fill your heart with goodness until it overflows and burst.

Try to share the goodness that flows inside of you, because even if you're broken God can fix that part too. He will pick up the pieces and gather them with love; and fill all the cracks with his supernatural love.

WOW!!!

How do I share that?

Often I wonder, how do I share what I'm feeling without appearing weak? Life kicks you in the teeth, literally at the wrong time. When you need to express yourself and how you are feeling, often it falls on deaf ears. I tried before more than once, but I was snapped at and accused of being a big baby. That really... hurt my feelings, because at that time I would have loved to have felt nurtured. However I didn't want to feel like I was a nuisance either. It really cut me very deep seeing that I was already feeling miserable, and my pain was obvious. Your insults you said were a joke, but why at my expense? When you're cruising in the boat of despair of your own, why shouldn't I capsize it as well, and call it a joke? Is it wrong of me to need to be sheltered, from time to time? Haven't I supported you always, when you needed me? Yet I get crude remarks, entitled jokes and told to suck it up. I'm really beginning to believe that maybe, I can't trust your feelings for me. I've been told that life is the best teacher, and after awhile some things will start to sink in. I realize how easy and effortlessly you callously put me down and call it a joke. The real joke will be me that you lose when I turn away for good. Still I wondered why I stayed so long, now that I have decided to move on, laughingly now...how do I share that.

Terry E. Lyle

Tears

Why do you cry, and how does it make you feel? Tears of joy I understand completely. Tears of grief I offer my sympathy, as it saddens me as well. However, explain the tears that are shed because of unwise decisions. Why do you cry? Is it because you felt stupid or embarrassed over your choices, that no one could have stopped you from making? Do you cry because someone has hurt your feelings, or because you let yourself down and everyone knows about it? Crying your eyes out, should be worth something. Your tears should be replaced, with a cleansing healing effect. An awareness of what should be done next, while moving onward and forward. Sincere tears flow when your soul which has been bruised, obviously no longer can contain the emotional baggage. Your internal wounds bleed the salt of your tears. Guttural cries are extremely painful; it's that low point of realization, that's too sharp to digest. Then there are tears of trickery. Those types of tears can be turned on or off at will and usually stop as soon as what's requested or desired has been achieved. The sad and salty, simmering on and off for days type tears, where your eyes stay swollen, you lose your appetite, and you retreat from life's activities behind closed doors; those tears are the most heartfelt. Instead of giving you tissue, I'd like to give you my shoulder to lean on; while keeping you in prayer, because "prayer changes things."

Teenage Years

I'm sure you don't understand why there are rules and expectations from your parents. The reality is that you're trying to live in a world without rules and accountability. You sit back and allow your parents to feed and clothe you. You don't have to like your parents, but you have to deal with them, this is all you have. The kids today think they know everything, but they will have a hard life ahead of them. They have only been on the planet a few short years in the scheme of things, but they believe they know more than the matured adult. I have grave concern for our children today, they have this medical problem called I won't listen, and last word syndrome. The pregnancy rate is soaring, transmitted venereal diseases are alarmingly high, and national academic scores are poor to average. The blame can be placed on parents as well as the child, because we all have been shuffled in this game called life.

Confusion

I find myself in the middle of confusion where I don't want to be, but I'm here never the less. My emotions are raw and brittle from what I hear and see. I'm stuck at someone else's crossroad. I wait for clarification of the mental mind games, lies, and deceit. The phone is never answered unless prompted by guilt or need. I tell myself that there is a pot of gold at the end of the rainbow, but, in getting there, I have to travel across mine fields with damaged carcasses spewed everywhere in sight.

I wonder if the journey is worth it. Little voices in my head send off radar warnings that I ignore in haste because I don't want to perceive it as confusion, yet I wonder whether I've made a mistake. It's too late to turn back because I've invested my heart into this tug–of-war, emotional roller-coaster. I find myself afraid to take a new chance on someone else, because their baggage would add to my already confused state. Yet, inside I feel deprived and overlooked. Have I wasted my time? This is the question unanswered with conviction I don't feel stirring within me.

Many nights alone my anticipation has been peaked of what I should do next. How do I step through the confusion to get to my pot of gold, at the end of the rainbow or is this another disaster unfolding? No one wants to be alone, but there is peace, mingled in sadness at the thought. Until there is clarity of what I stand to gain, or how long this journey will last, I find myself caught in a realm of confusion; alone and guarded for what's next. Tomorrow holds no promises, except someone will be part of some type of confusion, like me and like you. What should we do with this information? Should we dismiss it as unnecessary confusion?

Medicated

You need to be medicated before I can deal with you, because when you aren't medicated you act like a fool. Talking with you requires some work, because you either talk like you're stupid, or act like a jerk. Your highs and lows are scary at best, but with that nonsense; you need to put it to rest. Talking to you makes me shake my head; you will go on and on when you should go to bed. I don't know why you would miss taking the medicine you have, because when you do, it's a problem, and a pain till it passes. When I don't listen to your ranting and things, you consider me to be the vilest and meanest being. Your perception is screwed and you know that is true. It is the reason your doctor thinks you need the medicine too. On a good day when you've had your pills and a nap, it's on those days that we can talk, sit, and shoot the crap. So stay medicated and do what you do, so the normal people like me, can deal with confusing people like you.

A letter to my daughter

I'm in the age of this computer technology and I've just received an E-mail from my daughter. My daughter asked me, "Why did my grandmother help raise me and why were you gone most of the time while I was growing up." My daughter was also curious about her mom because her memory appeared foggy. She wondered when we changed from friends to foe. With a loving and humbled heart this is my letter to my daughter.

 I started by saying, "Baby I'll do my best to answer your questions, so that you may have some understanding and clarity. Yes when you were young I worked a lot, to provide what I thought you needed. Mostly to have you live in better neighborhoods, and keep you away from drugs and scary individuals' that is why I worked so long and so hard. I realized mostly that I saw you when I was standing over your bed while you laid in slumber. I've always paid more than what was reasonable for your childcare, because I could afford it, and thought it would be the incentive for them to provide better care in my absence. I brought you the best in clothing and jewelry, because that's how much I loved you. That's also the reason you were born, because I wanted and needed someone to love."

Terry E. Lyle

"When I was growing up, I didn't always understand the strict and harshness I felt from the parenting that I received as a child. I felt misunderstood and lonely, while very apprehensive of messing up and not measuring up. When I was a Paramedic, I received an emergency call for a sick child that turned out to be for you. I feared that the babysitter's sons were doing something perverted to you, and/or molesting you due to the nature of the call. That was the reason I let grandma watch you, because I knew you would be safe. The reason I left town and moved to California, was because when I was employed as a Correctional Officer, I was used as a decoy to get an escaped convict back into custody. I began to receive death threats against me and my family. I moved the furthest away from Baltimore to protect you and my family and keep you safe. I believe like anything else that through your teenage years, you were trying to grow up and exert your independence."

"You no longer wanted to share your thoughts with me, and the distance between us grew. I always felt comfortable with the responsibility of taking care of you but you wanted more freedom without understanding the consequences of life, that through my mistakes, I tried to shield you from."

"Even though it appeared I held on too tight, I just didn't want you to fall into the traps that I had fallen into. I always stayed in close proximity, just in case you needed somewhere to run, also, I didn't want to lose the best thing in my life, which you are. I needed to be the type of mother with whom you could discuss anything that you feared, regardless of what it was. I wanted you to know that talking to me would always be alright. I wanted the best for you, my beautiful black baby, and I did whatever I could to provide that. So honey, hopefully, you will understand that you will have to learn, to see things with your heart and not always through your eyes, in order to really know what matters... and I believe that's when maturity starts."

What makes you a Man?

What makes you a man? It's not the fact that you do not have face or chest hairs, nor is it not because your voice has deepened. Becoming a man is because of wisdom, experiences, and maturity in adversities.

There are no classes on how to become a man, but there are good role models that you can use as an example for your life. To know humility is part of the essence a real man will display.

A real man doesn't find pleasure in the pain of others; a real man reaches out to bring you to your full potential. A real man can cuddle a child and embrace an adult in moments of anguish, yet be reassuring that you're not alone.

Real men learn from the disappointments in their own lives yet, vividly never forget the pain or struggles. Real men are level headed and step up to be a leader to others through wisdom gained.

Real men are slow to anger and willing to listen. Excuses for their behavior aren't blamed on liquids in a bottle, or intoxicants taken. Real men are accountable and make restitution when in error with dignity and grace, knowing it's their responsibility to set their standards high and above reproach.

WOW!!!

Real men function well in the job market and better at home, because he knows he is loved for the quality example he sets for the family around him. For the men who fall short they will have family issues and crisis, because the head of the family will be a knucklehead.

Real men embrace the teaching of fellow wise men, so they can enhance their own mental development in maturity, so their internal demons don't surface their ugly heads in his thought process.

It's essential for a man to gather all facts before blindly engaging in foolish conversations and becoming destructive to tender minds that perceive him as a figure head. These are the basic things it takes to be a real man.

I feel like I got played

You knew before I did that you were going to disappoint me again, and I feel like I got played. Emotional baggage piles up and you express concern saying I'll be there for you, yet you don't come, so I feel like I got played.

In my pain I've fallen to the deepest depths of my awareness. From your beginnings, I couldn't measure, nor find comfort in your failed expression of comfort. I'm ridiculed again because you shared in my humility; I feel like I got played.

Intimate details blow upon the ears of on lookers without my knowledge. My trusted friend has now exposed again; I feel like I got played. I wonder should I place a bubble around my heart and my emotions. Maybe I should become aloof and distant, while keeping my secrets to myself, because I'm tired of feeling like I got played.

WOW!!!

Ranks of the Homeless

Homelessness is a terrible thing. It's sad to know that life is so unbearable for some, while others have so much. They constantly struggle to wonder when will be their next meal, at the risk of eating the meals that they will find in the trash cans. You look around and see that the populations of children have grown in the unfortunate ranks of the homeless.

If you think about it, there are classes of homelessness; just like any economic class. Let me venture to say that the poorest class of homelessness is the ones huddled in any corner, sleeping on the street, finding shelter in doorways, when there is no room in the shelters to house them.

The next stage of homeless is the lower middle class. They are the ones who have been assigned space within a shelter. They are bounded by time restraints on their departure movements of leaving during the day and returning at night.

Moving up the chain to middle class would be the ones who own their vehicles in which they sleep. They become mobile during the next day. They also have accessibility to and from to locate venues to eat and bathe, while maintaining the illusion that all is well.

Terry E. Lyle

Now, the upper class or rich homeless persons are the ones living in someone else's home. They contribute nothing and consume all morsels of food around them. They pay no bills and run their mouths like they are entitled. They have the gall to act like they can sit on their lazy butts and watch you provide, yet beg for more. The mooching, snooty, upper class, don't even realize that they too are homeless individuals.

But to the true homeless, I pray that you continue and never grow weary, because a brighter day is coming. Just hold on to God's unchanging hand. He delivered me and he can deliver you from the bonds of despair and pain of regrets. Just stay strong and my friends, please that, will you never forget!

Being homeless

Being homeless can happen to any man, and because of my story I know that it can. Lost without shelter and nowhere to go, my daily struggle is the only thing that I know. I lost my job then my home went next. Things went bad so quickly, I thought I was hexed. When you look in my eyes, please don't see a bum; just see the worst that my life has become. I only wish I knew how to get back on my feet, my life is so bleak that I feel the defeat. It's hard to be hopeful when you've lost all you had. Today inside I only feel sad. I survive on handouts, as the people pass me by. I smile thank-you while inside I cry. I've heard that brighter days are coming, and I hope that will be, because right now being homeless is all that I see. Opportunities pass because of economic lost; can't even build on the skills that I have been taught. My clothes are tattered and worn straight through, no longer providing warmth, not even my shoes. I huddled up so tight, trying to keep myself warm, no space in the shelter living type dorms. The weather is threatening to be really bad; a plastic bag to cover me is all that I had. But I'm not discouraged and I look straight ahead, tomorrow might be my chance to secure me a bed. So today when I arise and look all around, I hope a warm bed is there to be found. I'm down on my luck and this thing is true, remember my story could easily happen to you.

Terry E. Lyle

Talking to Jesus

Today I talked to Jesus and this is what I said,
"Can you provide a roof over me with a nice,
warm bed?" I didn't hear the answer but things
went very well. I found a new dwelling, and
it was no longer a cell. The same day I was
released I had so many things to do. The only
person I could count on was Jesus, and you.
Being in prison has altered my life, because on
the inside you have to constantly struggle and
fight. Nothing is sacred and your mind you will
guard, can't afford to cave into those insidious
scars. You've made a mistake with the choices
of your past, as you run towards freedom very
fast. Now things are seen in a different light,
since you've found Jesus you do what is right.
Who would have thought from all that you've
done, that through your victory with Jesus all
has been won?

Thanksgiving

Inspired by the gospel and lives from the good book, is why Thanksgiving is a holiday that is never overlooked. I'm talking about the bible so as we take a closer look, let's keep remembering the Passover before Jesus' life was took. All around the world people begin to reflect, thinking about a memory that often comes flooding back.

Families come together to share their time in love, being grateful for the blessings which come from above. The bounty is plentiful and it fills my heart with glee, smelling aromas of foods which are chasing after me. Hoping that on this special day, this Thanksgiving we will help the homeless, instead of pushing them away.

"Can you pass me the sweet potatoes, and yes I would like some turkey too? Can you give me a big heaping pile of macaroni and cheese, because I know I want that too?" There's roast beef, cranberry sauce, even chitterlings to name a few, food is so plentiful with choices, and I don't know what I should do. I need to save some space for my collards, stuffing, and pies.

After eating a feast like this, I would be in hog heaven with a smile. Think about your blessings and remember the things that you stand to lose, when there are people out there who wish they were in your shoes. God so loved the world that be gave his only begotten son, for whosoever believed in him, would not perish, but in victory life is won.

When we accepted Jesus and we invited him in, now because of his life that he gave, he cleaned us from sin. Proof of his deity he left on that very same day, when Jesus died, he ascended from the grave. So Thanksgiving day started a long time ago, it didn't start with pilgrims, and this we should know.

Christmas

Christmas time is finally here and I know my gifts are near. They will be wrapped beneath the Christmas tree, and piled so high this year. Wonderful caroling outside my door; I am so excited that I want even more. Fill my mug with eggnog and rum, and a slice of fruitcake because I want some.

Everyone is happy and filled with cheer, just because Christmas time is finally here. This year I'll be playing Santa, and that is a fact, I have my red suit hanging and my funny red cap. I won't come down the chimney, with my bag that's full of toys; times have really changed now...so I'll be coming through the door.

Santa will have many stops that he will have to make, so you can go to sleep now sweetie, don't worry and don't wait. I promise I will be there and I promise I won't be late. When you wake up in the morning, there won't be any mistakes. You will know that I came by in the middle of the night; seeing all the pretty gifts I wrapped in paper that sparkles in light.

I hope you are very happy during this Christmas time of year. I'm sending you all the cheer I have and wishing you, a Merry Christmas and a happier New Year.

Terry E. Lyle

If I Were Wealthy

If I were wealthy, this is what I would do. I would
wine and dine you, and take off your shoes. I
would massage your feet ever so nice, while your
drink of choice is smoothly, chilling on ice. I
would buy you everything that your little heart
desired. While inside my heart I would also fan the
fire. The love we would share would be awesome
to see, as I gaze at you and you at me. It's beyond
compare, to each our souls we would often share.
Time is endless when you are near, I feel like I
brought infinity, because you are here. If I was
wealthy this is what I would do, I would buy the
universe and give you that too.

Going through something

Going through something is a powerful statement. Everyone at some given time is going through something. Especially difficult is the fallout from mistakes generated by you. I physically feel sick on the inside, my head begins to explode. I think about the disrespect that others inflict upon you, because you allowed it by not saying anything sooner. Women should be treated like precious jewels, until you find out that their worth is nothing but glass then you can treat them accordingly. Sexually their purpose was to hold your liquids, because they lowered their standards to accommodate your lies. Up until that point, the highest form of flattery was attention with a hint of decency, when I should have demanded respect. I never considered myself to be overly enthralled into sports, but I find myself mentally jumping hurdles all the time. It's a great start however to recognize the problem, but then the follow through can make going through something difficult. The cliché, "if it isn't one thing, it's another", has become to mean, "If it isn't one thing, then it's the same thing over and over again". I finally figured this thing out. Human beings are supposed to go through things. That's how life works; things changing and evolving, yet basically the same. After all aren't we all going through something?

Who's in charge?

Have you ever really taken the time to look closely at relationships from the inside? I was thinking over the things shared by me and my lover. Wondering how often was I stuck on stupid, and why did things escalate so quickly into a mess. Well it turned out to be a reality check for me, as I thought things over. I would often relinquish my power with misgivings for the sake of love, letting them have control over minor decisions on which I didn't agree.

  I should have defended and controlled my own choice. Now that our relationship is strained I decided too late that no one should be the dictator of mutual decisions; it's just two lives shared by two. Mixed emotions now driving me crazy, wondering should I or shouldn't I let go. I have created a monster by not speaking up. Conclusion to my story: take charge of your life and share the love without resonating into despair over the bad choices, and know that you are in charge of you.

Sensuousness not Lustfulness

I've been called nasty, and sometimes a freak. It seems that when I am near you that my body is on fire. I close my eyes and run to a place in my imagination, where you can't find me.

It's sensuousness not lustfulness. I think about the heat of your body against mine. It's so hot yet doesn't burn to touch. My body starts to marinade at the closeness of your presence.

I slowly take my leg and rub it against yours and linger there. The tingling of my inside is like explosive impulses running towards the inner layer of my skin. Pounding against my flesh to escape but it isn't lustfulness it's sensuousness.

I close my eyes and take a breath and can actually feel the slowing of my heart. While the beats are rhythmically dancing to a sensual beat of their own, as I watch from a distance. I find myself gladly trapped in this world that is filled with you.

We are on center stage where you have the leading role. Our lives and bodies intertwine as we sway to the heat of our passion. I call this sensuousness not lustfulness. Every time I think of you my body becomes moist, but this is sensuousness not lustfulness.

My sister Sylvia

Sylvia is my sister that I wish could be here, even though we argue and fuss I still hold her dear. Many times in the past, do you know what Sylvia would do? She would get on my nerves and beat me up too. I remember the fights that we used to have...she was thumping on me while kicking my ass!!! But I would fight dirty when I was losing my grip; I remember biting her hard on one of her tits. As sisters we weren't really very close, and getting on her nerves I did that the most. Sylvia has a soft spot for me and this I do know, even though she hides it and won't let it show. There are some other memories that I will share with you. I remember the day when I put a snake in her shoe. I knew fighting her trifling tail I didn't want to do. I laughed so hard that it really made me cry, I was pissing, bent over, laughing, and holding my side. Sylvia always blamed me every time things went wrong, but I don't know why, because I was usually gone. Whenever she tried to sneak out late at night, I would squeal on her tail and start a new fight. The struggles with Sylvia have all been up hill, but that heifer will receive some money when I die in my will. I love my sister and that is true, but tormenting her is just what I do!!!

My brother Stanford

I have a brother named Stanley, but we call him Stanford a lot.
He's the one I need whenever I get in a fight. He's the strong silent type and don't say very much. But if you pick on his sisters, I
think he'll whip your butt. He's my mother's oldest child and that
will say a lot, he would wash the dishes including all the pots. He
was the one who would steal my candy, when I would tell him
no. Stanford would beg for my sweets while stepping on my toes.
Now sometimes he would help me, a little or a lot, he would even
tie my shoes into the ugliest little knots. Or sometimes he would
bully me and try to beat me up. But sister girl handled herself
and she knew what she needed to do. One day this fool he spit
in her face, and I really lost my cool. I was on him like a cheap
suit and I had no time to waste. I was so mad at my brother that I
jumped all in his face. I was so angry I thought that I would bust,
I believe on that very same day that I quickly learned to cuss.
Yeah my brother was tripping; he had to have lost his mind. That
was a nasty thing he did, and I jumped on that behind. I remember another time that I also got him back, plus it really made me
laugh real hard that I got a pain in my neck. He stole my cookies
one day and I responded to that real fast, so you know what I
did to him? "I really cracked that ass!" I took a coke soda bottle
and whacked him on his head. He now has this permanent scar
that's so noticeable, that he'll wear it until he's dead. My cousin
Little Bill was watching us and even he had to laugh. Even though
he spanked my butt; he smiled and said "girl you are really bad"!
The moral of this story is that you deal with the family that you
receive. Nobody else really wants you, and that you can believe!!!

Terry E. Lyle

My brother Phillip

I have a brother named Phillip and he's a big old ham. Wherever you might see him, there's a camera in his hands. There are so many things that I would love to talk about, never bring drugs in his house, or he will throw you out! Now Phillip is a really great cook and has some awesome skills. When he asks if I want him to fix my meal, I say "certainly if you will." His creations should be in a book, because he really has some flair; the things that he thinks of, is like pulling it from the air. The meals that he fixes are definitely quite a feast. When you hear the clanking sounds of utensils then everyone wants to eat. People come from all over from his tiny little town, when they hear he's cooking and laying the portions down. Now Phillip also has a temper that you don't want to see. His veins will pop out and the fire in his eyes starts billowing. That's a scary sight that truly has also frightened me, and if it's like I remember I definitely don't want to see. Now I remember when I was small and got on his very last nerve. Many times I had to run to my momma so my life she would preserve. But now we are both grown up, and we are the best of friends, that share a special bond that I hope will never end. My love for my brother Phillip it grows stronger day by day. So I smile when I think of him in that weird and crazy way.

Commitment

You ask me to be your girl, and you want a commitment in our relationship. How long have I waited to hear those words? Now bitter-sweet, I wonder why now? I still love you, that haven't changed. Was it your fear of losing me? Or did you want a security blanket, to the choices pressing in your life? Be honest with me, why now? Freely I accept your offer, as I've so often did in the past. Is this wise, to abandon my carefree lifestyle to be committed to you? My heart says yes, but my brain tells me to slow down, and think this over. I crave the closeness and warmth of your touch. I look forward to the twinkle in your eyes, as I listen intently for the sound of your voice. My heart skips when you are near. Why would accepting this offer appear to scare me? Is this not what I ultimately wanted? Now the fire's lit. I'm afraid to get burned, and I fear that maybe I should retreat. There's no comfort zone to run to. I need to be loved, so why can't I trust love to come in? Can it be that when I extend love, its' internal and it dictates what I do by my actions so that it'll release me from the words, I'm committed?

Terry E. Lyle

After the tub

Butt naked again, lying across the bed looking up at the ceiling. What is it about me not wearing clothes that excites me so much? The naughty thoughts appear decadent in my mind. I love the coolness of the sheets against my warm flesh. I feel like an animal that can run free without reproach. Playfully I roll over and over, amusing myself. Tenderly I trace my leg's outline upwards towards my belly button. I poke my finger in and out of my navel to feel the suction motion on my finger tips. I arch my back in the air to take that long delightful stretch. I slowly spread my legs open, as a rush of cool air blows over my hidden treasures. Steam surrounds my neck from the inferno of heat within me. Suddenly upon my skin, a droplet of moisture escapes me. How blissful and exciting it feels. While lying in my nakedness, I think from this moment on, that I will utterly refuse to wear clothing. I was happily dancing around, when I noticed someone behind me with their hands on their waist. "Stop messing around and dry off, It's time to go little girl, so hurry up and put your clothes on!!!"

WOW!!!

Nasty Stuff

Have you ever gotten tired of someone talking dirty, sharing dirty pictures, and always ignoring your plea to not share this with you? In the gutter their mind stays, never wanting to look up and see daybreak. The dark side of humanity grips at your insides in a lustful manner. Have you wondered if this is a new Sodom and Gomorrah? Sin cities are popping up everywhere, so why do I need your filth dumped in my yard? Am I intrigued by the awakening of impulses in my body while secretly I want you to continue? Or do I want to overload my impulses with your graphic innuendos and ignite the stuff in me... that's nasty?

Money doesn't make you!

Money doesn't make you, but money can break you. It can take you places you might not want to go. Money should be put somewhere inside of a bank as your dividends slowly will grow.

Money can pay your many expenses; also build up walls of paranoia, while making you defensive. Start by creating a nest egg for your future, so the life you want to have will pleasantly suit you.

Money is the reason that most crimes are committed, some lazy people won't work hard to get it. It's a struggle trying to build your wealth, working long hours and affecting your health.

Money won't make you any better than me, you've just been afforded a different opportunity. If you mess around a little too much and think that you're grand, that money can slip away, like sand through your hands.

Looking for Daylight

High again and being unreasonable, you're mad because you're broke and there is no one to loan you money. Craving the drug that makes you paranoid, talkative, and in some cases, unable to talk at all, because of dry mouth and a tongue that has been numbed.

Your clothes are wrinkled, make-up smeared or overdone, teeth yellowed and your breath stinks and your fingernails are dirty, but this doesn't matter as long as you have the money or drugs with which to get high.

You are rushing to the drug man to get a fix. Once you've bargained for the fattest bag of crack, concealing it as if it were gold, you peek around to see if any police are near, then you scurry off to the place where you can get high.

In your mind you make a mental checklist of all the supplies which will be needed, as you visualize what is handy. "Yes I have my smoking pipe, copper chore, lighters, cigarettes, alcohol, mirror, razor blades, baking soda, and spoon."

Excited to know the fun is about to begin, you can't wait to get high, as you feel the tingling of anticipation of your first hit. You put your mirror down first so you catch the drugs from spilling onto the floor.

You open the valuable containers holding the drugs, while you look around to make sure all doors are locked and no one can see who isn't invited to the feast of madness.

A hush comes over the room as the smoke billows in the air, from your first intake and release of the crack cocaine, exhaled from the overflow of the lungs. Your head begins to spin as sweat flows from your brow. Your heart races and you think, "Wow that was a good hit" then you cough because the excess of smoke in your lungs didn't go down the right pipe.

Initially you think of the calmness your body now feels, only to later have it replaced with paranoia at every sound that you begin to hear. As sirens blare in the distance, you rush to peek out of the window, hoping it's not the S.W.A.T. team waiting outside to kick the doors in and bust you on a drug charge.

Now that your drugs are finally gone, and your pockets are empty, you begin to aimlessly look around on the floor. You hope to find even the smallest piece of crack to smoke, picking up lint and trash as you taste it, and spit it out, realizing your last hit is over. You feel stupid and disgusted over how you've wasted your money.

Over and over again you seek out anything resembling a piece of drug. Flustered, your pockets are empty and you're left with a nasty taste in your mouth. In this sobering moment, you realize this madness and constant nightmare can't continue.

Thinking about how you would have to dodge the police, while chasing down the drugs, you become ashamed of resorting to lying, stealing, or begging, and acting like a fiend for drugs in your brief moment of lucidity. You shake your head and wonder "When will I see daylight"?

WOW!!!

The birth of a child

The birth of a child is a wonderful thing; the ability to carry life will make your heart sing. A miniature person you will create, whether they will come early or whether they come late.

While inside your belly you feel the fetus grow, wondering what look their little faces will show. The stages of growth within your womb are the most important things, while keeping your diet very interesting.

Loving and precious are what all babies are, the look on those faces when they are sweet and so small. That is what makes having them the most precious of all. They smell so fresh while cuddly and soft; in love with them, you will find yourself lost.

You bundle them up so as to keep them warm, protecting the babies from different weather type storms. A new life, if you are blessed to have, is an extension of you that will always last. Whether they are biologically yours or rather you're just raising a crew; they still will become the very best part of you.

The birth of a child is a gift from God. Train them wisely with a loving rod. In the direction that you want them to grow, so that important life lessons they will always know.

The birth of a child will have you buying so many things, showering them with gifts as if they were kings. You will plan the colors to paint their room, which is filled with sunlight and marshmallow moons. Colorful rabbits, and brand new things, are some of the stuff which will become their favorite things.

You are counting the days until the baby arrives, with occasional mood swings that will make you cry. There are swollen bellies and swollen feet; as most pregnant women will take all the seats. But when the day comes that the baby appears, all around will be sounds of cheer.

The birth of a child is a joyous thing and hope for the future is the blessing they bring.

It's time to let go

I find myself sitting here beating myself up as I wonder, "why do I stay in this dysfunctional relationship." Many times when things didn't go right I just chalked it up to the little bumps along the way. In my disappointment I took a very long hard look at what I expected and needed in this relationship.

What I realize was that I was just comfortable having someone interested in me. I felt usually disrespected or overlooked by you, but when kind words and respect came from another, I wondered why I wasn't receiving this from my significant lover.

I guess I fell into the trap where I exposed my heart and then allowed others to see me as vulnerable since they know I'm longsuffering, and they constantly take me to my limits; hoping that a kind word here and there will put things back together.

The moment has arrived that I think it's time to let go, while I continue walking and hoping for the best. The reality of the situation no longer works for me, when I finally faced some hard truths. It's been such a bumpy ride, that I think it's time I give it a rest and it's time I let go.

Terry E. Lyle

Eyes

What lurks behind my eyes when I look at you? I see every-thing, while looking for nothing, yet searching for truth.

Small things escape my mind, yet what's ugly and insightful I usually remember. My eyes tear up when I listen with my heart and not my ears. Sometimes they tear up when dust is near.

My eyes hold the responsibility of logging information of life. Remove my sight and those images move to the brain for catego-rizing. My eyes show warmth, fear and love.

My eyes are always under a covert mission, seeking out and aware of danger. My eyes show amusement when caught off guard. My eyes are brown but on some days feel blue.

My eyes also tear up and water over you.

I'm a Big Girl Now

I'm a big girl now and on my own. I'm a big girl now and fully grown

I have a husband and two young kids, sometimes I feel like losing my mind, while grabbing my head

I'm a big girl now and problems to boot; I'm a big girl now, still working to save the loot

One day I'll leave away from here, and I'll find myself free of fear

I'm a big girl now, in love with someone else, I'm a big girl now, and I need to live life for myself

I'm a big girl now, please don't tell me what to do; I'm a big girl now, if you try to regulate me, it's not going to happen I assure you.

I'm a big girl now who has to fill my own shoes, I'm a big girl now and my path, I'll choose

And when I'm upset at night, with the terror of things that aren't quite right, then I'll remember this little thing, when the little girl inside of me who in fear she clings to the thought that, "I'm a Big Girl Now."

Terry E. Lyle

Where do we go from here?

How many times did you say we were through? Even though you knew I loved you; where do we go from here?

How many times did you tell me to go away? Even though you wanted me to stay; where do we go from here?

How many times did you beg me to stay? Even though you were unfaithful anyway; where do we go from here?

How many times did you say you loved me? And promised to stay for eternity; where do we go from here?

How many times was I a shoulder to lean on? But when I needed you, you were always gone; where do we go from here?

How many times are you going to let me down? I'm on an emotional carousel turning round and round; where do we go from here?

How many times are you going to play with my heart? Chipping it away in small little parts; where do we go from here?

How many times do I have to fight with you? I'm trying to save a relationship I don't want to lose; where do we go from here?

After giving it some thought I'll take your heart, even if you give me the smallest part, because without you honey; where do we go from here?

WOW!!!

Running Things

I have this habit of running things; I have been told, I really don't do it because I am old.

I'm always trying to suggest doing a thing this way and that, I tend to rub the nerves and that is a fact.

I love order in my life and I focus real good. I try to do the things that I know I should.

So take a step back and look thru my eyes, it's not running things, it's just being wise.

I'll try to remember when stating my case, to sprinkle my wisdom with a little more grace.

Terry E. Lyle

Fear

Fear is dark and intense; it will make your heart race and chills will penetrate you down to the bone. Cold sweats will have you cringe as you seek a safe place, while in your fears you have been engulfed. Your mind is racing a thousand miles a minute, wondering what you should do next. Your breathing is rapid and your hands are clammy, while the look in your eyes exposes your fears. When all fear really is basically just (Facing Events and Realities).

Friends

Friends that you think you have are sometimes the people who you can really do without. They are full of themselves with the crap that they speak; they get on your nerve and make your brain weak. You become exhausted trying to make them understand that their silly ideas aren't the greatest of plans. While they make excuses for the things that they don't do, while their crazy behinds want you to believe awful dumb stuff too. Have you ever noticed that they won't be honest at all with themselves, but will lie like dogs from those stories, from what I can tell? It doesn't take a rocket scientist to figure this thing out. You can expect a story from them clearly without a doubt. Sometimes they will try to turn on you, because they can't stand to hear the truth; even when they know that it is completely true. Their lives are a mess and their acquaintances are few, people don't want to deal with them because of the crap that they spew. Their feelings get hurt real easy and they become so sad, but inside all you feel is disgusted and mad. They will have you wasting your time, trying to help figure them out, while they fuss and complain and verbally want to fight. So you stop calling them for awhile because you really need a break, but here they come approaching you with another intense headache. In every conversation you have, you always have to explain; they take everything so personal, while the drama they gain. Life is so simple; and occasionally there are some ills, but they can work your nerves some days that you sometimes desire a pill. Everyone isn't the same and I know that this is true, but why complicate it with dumb stuff that's not even true. It's not important to be the one who is right, just learn from the facts and try to stick it out. Be grateful that you both aren't foolish and learn what you can use, this is what people do and it's the basic rule. Maturity comes from the mistakes that you've had, so when someone shares with you, don't become so mad; just use what you can use. Take the advice in the spirit that it's given; a friend is trying to help and share some thoughts that are hidden. They are there to support you always having your back, so stop your tripping and just clearly hear the facts. Or you can continue doing things the way that you used to do, live life full of chaos usually generated by you! You're miserable, alone, and completely by yourself, because the choices that you've made aren't really the best. Have you noticed that nobody really wants to deal with you, could this be the indication why your friend list is few? When you hear things that you don't want to hear, try not to take it so hard, just make the adjustments and drop the silly façade.

Grapes

I love grapes, the red seedless are the best. It's like eating candy without gaining the extra weight. The way I pop them in my mouth I don't even hesitate. I would have a big bowl of grapes and a smile on my lips, as soon as they touch my tongue on the slightest little tip.

Sometimes I would cram them into my mouth and my cheeks would begin to bulge, but I couldn't stop eating them… until I ate them all. Some people like the green grapes, but they don't work for me, even those huge globe grapes with the seeds that you can see.

Now I have tried that black grape, that puckered up my lips, they are really good for cooking and that's a little tip. I know you appreciate your grapes If you like to drink your wines, but how you consume your grapes to me is just fine. I wish I had a grape vine, right in my own back yard. I could pluck and eat my grapes, and turn into a wad and watch the grapes turn into raisins when they get hard.

Terry E. Lyle

Broccoli

I was lying across my bed eating some broccoli, when all of sudden this thought came immediately to me.

I visualized being a giraffe which stood high over top of the trees, as I continued munching, on my bushy, treelike broccoli.

Giraffe's are very tall and eat from the top of the trees, so that's why I felt like that beautiful tall animal as I ate my broccoli.

When I wondered why a giraffe would decide to eat a tree, then a light came on inside my head when I looked at my broccoli.

I smothered it with butter and a tiny pinch of salt, and I ate till I was full and I practically ate it all. I've finally got my intake of vegetables that I really knew I needed, but if I had listened sooner, those warnings I would have heeded.

I was told that broccoli was a really good food to eat; it also helps with the swelling, which accumulates in my feet.

Broccoli keeps my system cleaned, while receiving those fibers that are edible and so green. Broccoli provides a lot of nutrients, good for you and me to digest. There are so many ways to prepare it, but I like it plain, salted, and buttered the best.

WOW!!!

Some people like their broccoli smothered in cheese, but when it comes to my broccoli, I just ask for a little more please. Now I need to run to the grocery store and buy these tiny little trees, packed in some plastic, this veggie called broccoli.

Terry E. Lyle

Opinions

It's my opinion that how you feel about yourself should be what counts; don't think that you need to be validated by other's opinions.

We all have opinions, but are you true to yourself? When the ax falls, you will have to be accountable for your actions and reactions.

Never be afraid to step out on faith and try new and different things. Life is so beautiful when you slow down and take a look around. It's my opinion that you should enjoy every minute of it.

When the grim reaper comes for you, there will be no "Do over's" or "Wait a minutes" available to you, so make your life count. Feel life while you see life in its spectrum of colors, people, and stimuli.

When you look in the mirror, see the beautiful person you are and can be. Bring to the surface the qualities of compassion and humility, then love I'm sure, will spill out of you.

But this is just my opinion!

Facing the facts

It's time I start facing the facts I'm in a relationship filled with hot passionate explosive sex, yet the reality is that it's heading nowhere. I'm in love with this man whom I believe loves me, but I'm stuck in the middle of a triangle. I supply the romance and the he supplies the finance. The struggle is whether I should continue doing wrong, with no proof that I won't come out of this mess unscathed. I continue knowing that this relationship might cause possible long term damage to my soul. As I ponder over the realization that we are great together in numerous ways, the sex is just the icing on the cake. I think, "When should I start facing the facts"? In my partner's defense or guilt, he reminds me of the shameful acts we are committing. When I want to live in the moment, I close my eyes and I visualize the laughter and silliness we share. I gasp for air as I relive the moments of his tongue on my body and his touch skillfully caressing my soul. The fact still remains that I should really allow myself to be loved by someone available. It's time to stop hiding my affections behind closed doors and stolen moments. It's time I started facing the facts and set my lover free. When love is right, it will return back to me.

The Power of Love

With hope I press forward, in fear I step cautiously. With determination I overcome my struggles. In pain I continue, yet in love I rest.

I close my eyes to daydream for a moment. My focus seems to be all about you. In a trance like state, I'm driven to reach out towards you. Gentle whispers of air flow, delicately across the tips of my fingers. Soft and sensuous like your lips upon mine, I visualize your touch upon me while inside I whine.

Surrounded by the barriers I build about me, yet needing to peek out and join the world, I hide. Looking beyond my defenses, and willing to let my guard down, I invite and allow you to come in; to share the best part of me, that only a few will privately see.

Laughter and giggles of happiness, mingled with tears of joy and excitement, purge the darkest areas of my soul. In your smile I'm illuminated, but in your love, I am bathed. I have precious memories of the mind which has already been saved.

Insecure

My sweetheart is very insecure, never trusting the love that surrounds him. We all carry baggage from our past, yet his scars appear deeper than the smile resonating from his face. I wish I could take a trip into his past, and avenge the hurt afflicted upon him, while in his tender years. I would love to beat the crap out of the monsters of his past, and be his super hero. I would shed light upon his pathway, when the road he walks upon begins to darken. I would hold his hand when things are scary and he starts to slip. I would hug him tightly when he's cold within my grip. I'd like to be the one to fight the bullies off, and speak for him when his voice is humbled and soft. I'd like to be the one to take away his pain. I can't change his past, but I can change his today. Never will he have to be insecure about the love that is in me. I will share this love so freely and definitely so completely.

Terry E. Lyle

When I played cards on Christmas

I was playing cards all night long and I was winning, "Oh my God"! When my partner started helping the other team out, and screwed up our odds. I was thinking in this card game she should have been barred. I would roll my eyes and look at her mean, smoke was flaring out my nostrils in an ugly scene. I was thinking I wanted to whip her butt; I came to win not huff and puff. She was telling them things that messed up the odds, I was playing so good and I was playing real hard.

The other team started winning and laughing in my face, I needed to turn this thing around with no time to waste. Then the guy from the other team smirked and said with glee "Feliz Navidad" as he laughed at me. I rolled my eyes and said really quickly, "You can kiss my rump and I said it so slickly." They hollered in laughter at the top of their lungs, this card game for me had lost its fun. My partner said "why don't you calm yourself down", I looked at her with the meanest frown.

I was thinking, "I don't believe this crap; she is playing with me and should have my back". I started huffing and puffing and looking sad, my miseries of losing were making my opponents glad. We played cards until six a.m., and on the very next day, they brought their A game, when they came to play. You know I can't wait to play cards again and increase my odds because I came to win.

As luck had it a week later on New Year's Eve, we came to play cards cheerfully. My partner and I finally won. We roasted those butts till they hollered they were done! It's all in fun when we come to play, even though I will act like a fool when the game stops going my way.

Terry E. Lyle

The Pages of your Life

Living your life like it's golden, bright and shiny and new. Even thou the choices are yours, sometimes often hard to do. I'll pass on my wisdom, and share this with you. Always seek what's fundamentally true. Never restrain yourself when you should be enjoying yourself. When you take a trip, take only your luggage and leave your baggage behind. When you meet new people, try to be kind. Don't confuse yourself wondering about what others are thinking. Keep your life intact, and protect your spirit from sinking. You have a clean slate, you have erased the past, moving forward towards things that last. What you write down on the pages of your life should include God and that is nice. Live your life without regrets and you'll feel as if you've done your best. Make this journey an exciting lifetime of memories, ones that will last for infinity. If you are thought of and on someone's mind, then when they reflect on you, I hope the words are kind.

Trust

Trust is one of your biggest issues, also one of your hardest obstacles to get over. I understand you've been mentally violated, and your trust factor has been ripped right out of your heart. The damage was so intensive that you have blocked yourself from moving forward. Everyone is suspect and everyone has an agenda, but trust, I fear is not one of them. Your pain is inflicted on others because of your lack of trust. I've often wondered how something so precious and freely given could be so hard to recapture once set free? Trust bruises very quickly and its mark takes forever to heal. It lasts what seems a lifetime. You find yourself afraid to believe that you will ever find it again. Trust and people are like a flower pot full of weeds. The flower pot represents the trust that blooms within you. The weeds represent the people that have abused and choked the life out of your trust. Once you begin to pull out the weeds, you reveal the beautiful flowers that were hidden. Now maybe the qualities of trust can be watered and flourish again in you. If you nurture and set it free, then trust will find its way home, to the rose petals of your heart.

Terry E. Lyle

I Had

I had what I had before I met you. I don't need you to feel complete. I loved me before you even thought about loving me. I've always been complete, even thou you make me feel whole. I admit you touch something deep in my soul. I'm not impressed in the trapping and frills, before I met you I still paid my bills. I've always had style and a little flair, though I'm willing to let you pay to fix my hair. You can spend money on me, if you dare. Trust and believe I won't care. We complement each other in a very nice way, but when I'm mad at you I really don't play. The important thing that I see between us is that we love each other, even when we fuss.

I see a Blessing

Time and time again people are complaining about problems, when I see the blessings. Have you ever had car troubles that really agitated you? It appeared to be an unexpected issue, but you were able to finance the repairs. You had associates come to your aid and you're still safe; isn't that a blessing?

Have you ever gotten so agitated because something made you late for work? You were reprimanded for being late, but you still have a job; isn't that considered a blessing?

You're on a religious retreat and you have been notified that your home has been robbed. You see this as a problem but you weren't there to be injured in a home invasion, and the church has helped replace your belongings; this I see as a blessing.

You're sick, spending all day in the emergency room, hungry and tired and not feeling your best. This appears to be a problem, but you're alive and I see the blessing.

Upset and worried because there is no food in the refrigerator. This appears to be a problem until someone invites you out for a meal; in this I see a blessing.

Your heat temporarily went out and the weather is bad, but you have blankets and food while you wait on the technician. You're frustrated and see this as a problem, yet you're not suffering from hypothermia; I see the blessing.

Sometimes you're guilty of running your mouth, and making others around you very mad where they think about hurting you. Because of the power of prayer and restraint, they don't prey on you while they hold their peace; I can see this as a blessing.

A loved one has suffered for a long time and died, it's a problem wondering how you'll go on. Your loved ones are no longer in pain and they have left footprints on your heart, in this I can see the blessings. So whether you lack wisdom or not, when you think things can't get any worse, instead of seeing a problem, why don't you see your blessings?

The Cable Man

As soon as I can is what I heard, but that terminology is for the birds. It flies in one ear and out the next, while stuck on stupid with a pain in the neck. I've been waiting all day for you to arrive, and most of my plans have gone bye-bye

You never showed or made a call, to let me know you wouldn't arrive at all. Now I have to reschedule for a day that's free, to secure my cable for my TV. They don't care about how long you wait, and now the cable guy I really do hate.

My whole day was shot and I profited nothing at all, because the cable company refused to call. They could have told me that they wouldn't make it today, and I would have happily been on my way. Sitting and sitting while watching the door, no knock I heard while I paced the floor.

I have reception for a few channels on my TV, not that many, I think maybe just three. My wait was so long that I was mad as heck, if I was a bird, his eyes I would peck. I called on the phone to the cable company, when I decided to forget what they offered to me. And I will watch the few channels on my TV.

Terry E. Lyle

Victims

Have you ever considered yourself a victim? If not, let me enlighten you, because we all are victims? Identity fraud is chasing you down. Muggers lay in wait around the next corner, while vendors overcharge for merchandise, so we all become victims. Inside a relationship you're overshadowed by his dominance and idiotic behavior, while she cleans out your wallet in her sexy dance of seduction, making you as well, a victim. The word victim implies being taken advantage of while suffering through injury, mental pain, and or deceit. Sometimes our own pattern of indulgence makes us a victim to destructive behavior patterns. Wishing to flush out those undesirable thoughts and cravings make you a victim of lewd and decadent aspirations towards masturbation and sexual deviance. To some form or fashion, we all have become victims when, even our own vices have victimized us.

Controlling my Life

It's time I start controlling my life. I'm tired of different people dictating what I should do with my life. I'm an adult, but everyone wants to control my thoughts.

I wonder does anyone really understand how I feel. You might understand visually the torment associated with the lost of my freedom in choices. It's so precious to be able to have the luxury of choices. To snatch that away is grossly painfully tormenting, yet inside that's how I feel. I need to gain control over my life and the direction that it takes, living by the moments created by me. I've taken the low road and allowed this control issue to swallow and consume me into despair, when I should have been seeking the high road to possibilities. It's now time.... I started controlling my life.

I just don't know

I don't know what decision is better for the present or what decision is better for my future. This is my current dilemma; whether or not I should shut down the advice wagon. I've been accused of being bossy and judgmental, yet told that I'm intelligent, wise and insightful. Now along with those traits come confidence, foresight, and quick decision making skills. Presently I feel my brain is being picked like a ripe fruit, fresh on the vines, used to anticipate potential problems created by others. Now I don't mind sharing my wisdom however, it would be nice if it was taken initially instead of when the disaster strikes. The problem is that after I witness and assess troubles on the horizon I verbalize my warnings before being asked to do so; then I am accused of bossiness. So when I think that I'll keep my opinions to myself, then I'm accused of having an attitude. It seems I'm caught in a no win situation; darned if I do and darned if I don't. Someone needs to take the initiative and do or say what needs to be said, without reservation. Why wait until things have fallen down and you're caught in the aftermath, when basically, you need to step up? I don't know whether it's worth it to be stressed out and/or losing hair over someone else's problems or issues. Now academic smarts and street smarts are different and I'm pretty well balanced in both areas. Some individuals have too much academic sense and lack common sense. They talk themselves into their own reality, even when the facts are right before their eyes. If you were to see them on the fence, they are leaning so far over you would think they'd fall. However, the cleanup crew is usually the ones who are there to pick up the pieces; they are the ones grossly under estimated. That's when you are accused of being condescending, because you embrace your confidence of wisdom. What can I say, I just don't know? If others lack the speed of arriving at the same conclusions, should I become the target, with a bull's-eye on my back? I speak truth into existence...learned by life's challenges...while I struggle and shake my head because, I just don't know.

Terry E. Lyle

Wake up call

For months now I've listen to your complaining about I want a divorce. Yes you've taken the steps to secure an attorney, but really you don't want a divorce. Let me tell you why. Every time you have a whimsical moment of your past, you blame your husband, because it's now his fault because you didn't follow that dream. Over the years you find yourself clothed in the security of his presence. Love develops while yet unfulfilled, because you wonder back to the days of your past. Try hard as you might to verbalize that it's over, falls on deaf ears because you always end your conversation with "I love you back". Relationships with others are strained while they wait on a concrete decision on your part. To fall in love with you leaves you vulnerable to collateral damage. Locked into your past and refusing to press forward has your life in constant chaos. You have been loved by many, but you can't willingly commit your heart. Locked somewhere in your past it's time for a wakeup call.

Out of Control

Yes! I think you're out of control. Loud outbursts of emotions for no apparent reasoning; mood swings like jumping up and down on a trampoline, trying to balance your steps. I visualize you like a person running naked, with the wind in your hair, screaming, while waving your hands in the air all willy-nilly. As I think that I need to lasso you in and pull you back, I throw out the harness of comforting words, and you turn your head and growl. I back away cautiously, with conviction that it's no wonder that I think you're out of control.

Terry E. Lyle

Irritation

You make me irritated when I attempt to talk to you, unable to define my point of view because of your constant outbursts to talk over me; this is very irritating. In conversations that you agree to let some issues drop, then just seconds later you bring the subject matter up again and again; this brings me to the point of irritation. Every time when silence should be appreciated, you raise your voice so as to be noticed and heard in a conversation that should remain private; this I find irritating. I remember the good times that we have shared, even when there was nothing special planned. Oh how much fun we have had together, but unfortunately, when there is something specially planned, and people are in attendance, you show up and show out, and create any reason to cause confusion; I call this irritating. Forced to suppress your feelings in the presence of others, you remain in silence the whole ride home, then when we are alone, you want to be loving, and don't understand the cold shoulder; I find this irritating. When your problems or issues don't involve me, I jump to encourage you to higher levels of reinforcement and support, but when they do involve me, I treat you with respect and try to communicate with you in a quieter tone, so as not to bring attention to ourselves while addressing the issues. When I ask you not to show off in public at a public function, you insistently ignore my request with your loud outbursts and angry conversation. When you rain on my parade with your, "Me" victim speech over and over again; I find this irritating. Constantly you talk and never want to listen except to your own point of view. You snap at people, turn your head in disgust, and interrupt them loudly when they try to give their perspective, acting like a child who has to have everything their way; I find this totally irritating. True irritation is when I allow your negative behavior to continue. Eventually you will find yourself prematurely starting to gray from stress and agitation as frown lines start to creep upon your face. As you continue this vicious cycle without telling this person you've reached your breaking point, and you hold it in and physically upset your inner peace as you now have a constant headache; this I find to be irritating.

Terry E. Lyle

My Back

My back is in pain and I can't move very much, my pain is so intense that it hurts as I get up.

Being comfortable is a wish that I no longer have, because when I had some relief it never really last. I'm sick of where the pain radiates, and I can't get up very fast, but I have to do what I must do because this is the life I have.

My pain pills aren't effective and I don't know what I should do. I usually find comfort just lying in my room. I think my muscles have spasms and tighten up in a ball, and my body is hurting all over, trying to walk straight down the hall.

You don't have to be old to have trouble with your back; you could be young and still throw it out of whack. Heating pads or ice cubes whichever is your belief. I use them both, and they give great relief.

I start off with the ice so I can calm that puppy down; then I apply the heat until my pain can't be found. Now that my muscles can relax, I wait for the pain to subside, as I chill on my back.

The Silent monster

Please stop abusing the babies because it's so sad and makes me cry, when I see those precious tear stained eyes. I know they are being treated badly, whipped, and hit some adults are doing things that truly makes me sick.

Unfortunately it's sad to know that our kids are being abused by the ones who are closest to them. Parents call it discipline, yet they violently whip and beat on a child, leaving scars and memories of horrible nightmares. Unknown to most, they are the silent monsters.

Our children feel lost because there's no one to whom they can turn. It's even worse when the person who abuses them is family members and not the unknown predators. Scared and frightened while hidden and locked away in their minds, feelings of unworthiness attempt to shoulder the complexities of the why factor. They don't understand how one can love them, and yet treat them so cruelly.

This society has let our children down, leaving them unattended, and not watching for clues of their current discontentment. Our babies are victims of molestation, latch-key, physical abuse, emotional neglect, and provisional abandonment. In my soul I cry out at every bruise, every tear, and every lost life, because we failed to get rid of that silent monster that's preying on our kids.

Terry E. Lyle

These tender children are caught in a whirlwind of confusion, loneliness, and fear of being attacked again. They are power-less with nowhere to turn, but inwards, trying to find a reason to explain the madness. They don't understand why they feel unloved and a target of the abuse.

Our kids develop emotional instabilities; self esteem issues, and sometimes turn towards suicide. Some even evolve into another silent monster. It's time to break the cycle and save our children, before another one winds up dead at the hands of the silent monster.

Built for Comfort

Being overweight doesn't make you look bad, hold your head up and be happy and glad. It's not the outer appearance that makes you a star; it's your inner beauty that wins by far.

Don't worry about not being thin or built like a rock, because being built for comfort is what it's about. You are heat in the winter and shade in the summer, like a big classy car, you're built like a hummer.

Everything doesn't suit everyone, just handle your business and get your job done. You know the saying that you have a body by Fisher and a mind by Mattel, but I have a body built for comfort that makes the men yell, with alluring secrets but not show and tell.

And for some of you who don't know what that means, well Fisher makes cars and Mattel's a board game team. So your body might be built with a cute little chassis, but your mind is childish and as slow as molasses.

So you can think what you want about this big old body, but I caught you staring at me, because you know I'm a Hottie!

Terry E. Lyle

Flower pot relationships

Do you have a flowerpot relationship? Let me explain. Often I have been a witness to dysfunctional relationships. I've seen men controlling the thought patterns and decisions which should have been decided by both. Love in healthy relationships is evident when both are nourished and receiving the sunshine of hope, the wind of protection, and watered by the dewdrops of respect. Is your love relationship like a seeded plant, hidden within the soil, waiting to trust the journey to the surface where they sprout and grow? If your love interest is like a tree, tall and overshadowing, then it will block the things that are needed to grow strong and flourish. When both flowers receive the needed nourishments, they bloom in a beautiful array of colors that together, become a bouquet. Never let someone else's choices for your life become the status quo. Consider the source, review the advice then, decide what's best for you. Don't submit to someone else's will; stand tall on the truth. Compromise without being humiliated at your own expense; to please the idiocy of another should not be your focus. You have only one life to live, there are no do over's. You can bloom or perish, the choice is yours; however to bloom takes attention, time, and caring. Don't put all your focus into another, without making healthy choices for yourself. Become the beautiful flower you were intended to be and show your flower pot of humanity.

WOW!!!

Decisions

My decisions about you are usually made in my bed, that's where I think about things which dance around in my head. Sometimes I wonder if I should stay, or if I should go. Or should I have sex with you because no one would know. I have my secrets that are buried real deep, but when our souls merge, that is how we speak. How do I continue in the lies of deceit? When I hide my relationship while in slumber you sleep? I'm drawn away by the passions that I feel, you haven't satisfied me yet and I doubt that you will. A choice needs to be made, and I need to make them quick, because living this lie is making me sick. I'm tied up in knots and wonder what I should do; to me, I should be honest and accept what is true.

Remembering lost love

Good morning love,

Before I leave in a few moments, it was pressed upon my heart to share this with you. I know that I'm a chatterbox right now, but it's been years of conversations on which we missed out. In my excitement, I need to unload these feelings held deep within me, because there are so many things I want to share with you. First and foremost, I've always had that puppy love for you, sweet and unbridled. If you will allow me to call it that, I so admired you and still do. Today if you don't hear it, just know that someone still loves you, because I do. I'm as proud of the directions in your life, as I am for anyone who stays focused and gains success in their lives. To me, success isn't measured by the financial gains in your life, but by the inner peace you have. You illume a special calmness received because of your respect and integrity towards your family and peers. They see from your humility through your triumphs. To be honest, way back then, I admired you so much and still do, but I had an inner shyness, that I kept hidden because I was afraid to appear stupid. I need you to know today that I love you. Remember to always be good to yourself. Before I see my last sunset and blink my last eyelid, I smile as I remember the love that I lost. "MARANATHA"

Do you know Deborah?

Do you know Deborah, or do you think that you do? I know her well but what about you? Did you know she loves kids and she's very smart? While the love that she shows, flows straight from her heart. She always put God first, and that she will do..., but when you piss her off..., then she will step to you! She has good business sense that is beyond compare, and needless to say she is doing very well. Deborah thinks she can dance, while her stuff she struts, but I remember the old days when she and I cussed. She loves to play card games, but to win is a must. If you are her partner in spades, then in her you can trust. Deborah even tried her hand at writing poetry one day, but the last I heard they were all stashed away. Her poems are collecting dust probably in an old shoe box or two, hidden so deep from probing eyes from you. One special thing about my cousin that I will share, she is affectionate, funny and listens with care. Also a loving woman that knows how to cook, she has learned a few things from her recipe book. Her mom aunt Roxie shared all the wisdom she had, and because of that fact she didn't turn out too bad. Well the last and most important thing that I have to say. Is that "I love you girl and you brighten up my day!!!"

Terry E. Lyle

Why do I talk to you?

Do you ever wonder why you even talk to some people? I do and I've come to the conclusion that I must be a glutton for punishment. Talk about listening to those depressing, always nothing good happening in their life knuckleheads, drives me straight up the wall. I tell myself to treat them like soda's, not too many in a week or you'll break out. Listening to them would make an onion cry and ask to be medicated. There also are the loudmouths where you can't get a word in unless you have to scream over top of them to get your point across. Those are the ones with whom I need to have my earplugs engaged, so I can hum and nod like I'm listening. Oh let me not forget the big cry babies; they cry over everything and are so sensitive it just makes me sick of hearing the whining! It's like visualizing the cowardly lion in the Wizard of Oz, sobbing and holding his tail. Now let me not forget the bald-faced liars, the ones who have nothing coming out of their mouth that is truthful. It's just like being in the movies sitting there wondering what's next. If you thought I forgot about the perpetrators, wrong answer; they get on my last nerve as well. They always want something, while beating around the bush to ask for it. They act just like people with the jail house mentality; they build you up with concern for you before they imply they need something, and hope to trick you into volunteering to give it to them. When you least expect it, here comes those mushy I love you type telephone calls. Emotionally all caught up, you'll agree to anything, such as acting like an animal in a cage, going around in circles, waiting to be played with or shown some attention. Now I don't want to forget the ones who make me laugh; they are the bright side of my day. The only downside is that they will have you laughing so hard, your back will hurt and have you pissing all over yourself and make you wish that you were wearing diapers. Now how about the foolish ones that think they are like jets, straight up, but going nowhere, with their heads all in the clouds. I also can't forget about the ones who beat to their own tune, just plain crazy air heads with mental disorders. Let us not forget about those trifling people no one can get along with, they only call you because they have pissed everyone else off. Some people actually believe you are stupid with the rhetoric that comes out of their mouth, that they want you to believe; they are so transparent that you shake your head in awe, just listening to them. It's like looking through a glass house that you want to throw a rock through. So for all the thought that I've put into this statement just reaffirms the thought, "why do I even bother to open my mouth and talk to you?" Maybe I should learn how to use sign language; it'll minimize with whom I can communicate. So when I talk to you, I won't have to be irritated.

How do I go back?

How do I go back to the time when I wasn't so passionate or intense? How can I be less passionate, unless I learn how to love you less? You feel like we're at the crossroads of our relationship. You are afraid to venture forward because of the intensity of the ride. Safety equipment is needed to guard your heart, because turning your mind and heart over to someone else to nurture is foreign to you. Trust factors are limited by the damage of your past. You wonder how you can give away your comfort zone and allow someone else to reside there. How do I go back to the uncertainty of where I stand with you? Why do I want to drive myself nuts wondering if you love me completely, and if you are willing to share your life with only me? How do I go back to the time where you being mad at me didn't count? How do I turn off these nasty feelings inside, which are a result of the discord I feel between us? How do I go back to when I loved you less? Please tell me, how do I go back?

Since you've been Gone

Who would have known that since you've been gone, that I seem unable to function; I'm pretty focused and considered to be on top of my game. stripped of my pride since you've been gone, realizing nothing my dear really seems the same. My nights are longer, and time just trickles. My heart feels sad, while inside I cry. The pain grows worst, as each day drags. I still remember that beautiful smile on your face, the twinkle in your eyes, my heart can't erase. The laughter in your voice; rings sweetly in my ears. Small treasures like these, I truly hold dear. Impulsively I trace the outline of my body, where the touch of your hands, you used to caress. As I daydream how you were my best. You're the love of my life, in my mind that's clear. Honey I can't wait until you are here. To sum it all up, and to not make my story so long, I just needed to say this, since you've been gone.

Sweating me!!!

I hate when people are sweating me, pushy, obnoxious, and annoying chatter in my ear. Every day that you refuse is the same day they insist. People have the gall to make you feel bad about you telling them you can't help them today. This is what I call sweating me, it's when someone never lets up. Usually people who cannot accept no are the ones you should be on alert for, because they are part of the selfish majority. It is always their needs that take priority; fix their problem first and forget what you may be going through. You could be in pain, personal issues, or whatever. They don't care; they see only the small picture that doesn't include you. Wanting to borrow your car and you're low on gas, but you have enough to go where they want to go. I'll pay you later but later never comes, while now you're stuck. It seems that you have become always the contact person to everyone in need. When you lend out money, you have to struggle to get it back. The borrower wants to issue repayments in increments, not in the lump sum that you lent it to them. You are accused of sweating folks; how ludicrous is this? How can I be sweating you? The next time I have to go through drama to get my money back, I'll be sweating you with my fist upon your face!!! Once in need, will be in need again. When you have no one to turn to, then you will realize, after being pulled in several directions at once, with demands upon you, that's how it feels to be sweated.

The mess in my Life

As I look over my life and all the mess that I've been in, I can't help but thank the Lord from saving me from sin. I should have been dead... at least a couple of times before and with this thought, I am really...really... sure! I was hanging out in drug houses where I never should have been . I should have been flying out of those doors, but I was invited within. Other times in my life, I chose friends that I didn't need to have, because they encouraged me to do some things that I knew were really bad. I was trying to be grown and do all things my way, when I should have been taking advice more because, there were some serious consequences I finally had to pay. Silly things I remember about the stages of my life, some things were filled with horror and things that wasn't nice. I would listen to no one except to the garbage in my head, so you can imagine how I'm sleeping in this bumpy, rocky bed. You know what they say about the choices that you make; you sleep in the bed alone which were made by your mistakes.

Terry E. Lyle

Pain

Pain will make you realize things that your soul speaks to you. Pain also will make you do some of the things that you do. Physical pain I'm not speaking about, it's the mental pain that causes you to pout. It can be deep and very intense, while making you angry and on the defense. When you go through something which is emotionally hard, you lay around like a big lump of lard. Don't want to move or even react, your heart has been wounded and under attack. You need to stop and take a good look around. See the wonderful things in you which I'm sure can be found. Why don't you pull out the stuff crammed in the attic of your mind, to the basement of your heart, embrace the loving part of you, believing those things will never depart?

Broken Heart

My heart is broken as I cry over you; I cherished the love that I thought was so true. You have lied to my face, and you did it so quick. Now the thoughts that I have, they make me sick. Why did I believe the lies that you told? You promised me that together we would grow old. I should have known from your past that you and I could never last. I learned that passion without trust will only breed total disgust. You like the attention, while you're running your face, not realizing that you've hurt me so deeply and caused me total disgrace. My heart is wounded and it weeps salty tears, as I travel alone with uncertainty and fear. My heart is broken, and it's broken real bad, that I curse the memories…of you that I have.

Terry E. Lyle

Butt and Gas

Sitting on my butt and as wide as it is, I can't help but shake my head. Your butt may be narrow and it feels like sitting on a bone, or round and cushiony like a pillow at home.

The deal is really not that grand, we all will sit on our butts, when we hate to stand. If you exercise your butt and it looks really tight, I could imagine your clothes will look good by sight. Your muscles will be rippling all through your tail, not large like mine and shaped like a sail. Butts may come in various sizes, some you can hardly find, while others are huge surprises. As we sit, our butt cheeks spread out, then our butt cheeks wonders what that is all about. Some of you will be farting and trying to be slick, with that gaseous odor which will smell and make you sick.

Then you laugh like you're having so much fun, while everyone around you they start to run. So I'm going to squeeze my butt cheeks really tight, and hope my derriere looks good when I go out tonight. I'll wear my clothes just a little tight as my butt cheeks jiggle and jut out just right.

I hope I get the stares as I walk in a room, accentuating my buttocks while the people will swoon. Men will be saying that I have a nice derrière as I twirl around my butt in the air. Then I will so gracefully have a seat, so I can fart real quietly as I cross my feet. I will be hoping today that I don't have any gas, when I decide to sit....... on my voluptuous fat ass.

WOW!!!

Trying To Make It

Some days I wonder why I am trying to make it. When a problem enters your life it seems to come with a vengeance. Personally you have so many unresolved struggles to deal with while trying to fix someone else's as well. Pulled in many directions and filled with self doubt.

You don't want to give in to depression, yet you feel overwhelmed, and wonder how you can fake it. You put on a show that all is well when, inside you just want to give up, while craving for the intimacy attached with accountability of the presence of someone dear to you.

As you continue in the day to day routine you wonder, "Why me"? Crying doesn't help, yet you yearn for the release and peace of understanding. While going through the motions, you often wonder what your purpose is and would you be missed.

You fall prey to unhealthy relationships because you need to be needed, and desired, while you fight off the loneliness that knocks at your door. Many sleepless nights alone you listen to the creaking sounds of the night that haunts your inner being.

Tired of the bills piling up, everyone around you are either happy or complaining, while you feel empty inside and your only motivation for leaving is prior appointments made. You wish, "What would it take to disappear and start over unknown, somewhere else"? While you hope that your life's situations take a turn in a better direction.

When you realize the problem is you don't feel love, even though words have been expressed, yet still you don't feel the love. There is an emptiness that has grown inside, leaving you cold and abandoned to your own thoughts. The warmth of life seems fleeting. You hope that tomorrow, your thoughts aren't, "Why am I trying to make it."

Hiding

Locked up inside your mind, hiding from the cruel world out-side, you cradle your thoughts and insecurities; sadly putting on a front that all is well, while you crumble into shredded pieces of emotions, one more painful than the next.

Sorrowfully picking up the broken pieces to place back into the puzzle of your life, you struggle to continue. Fighting off temp-tations to self-medicate or self destruct, you press forward.

You need to be strong for others, but in your own weakness you wallow, like a bird whose wings have been clipped. Intimidation of failure running cold in your veins, you fake a weak smile.

Hidings from choices, letting others decide what's best for you, and not happy with their choices. You wonder are your feelings normal or bizarre, but yet inside you're hiding.

So stop hiding within your shell, a lot of us are waiting for your story to tell. As you take a deep breath and speak real slow, so we can receive your message that you want us to know.

When I woke up this morning

When I woke up this morning and jumped right out of my bed, I stood in front of the mirror and this is what I said. "Lord Keep me covered by your blood, and keep me safe today, so I don't constantly continue, making so many mistakes".

The plans that I have made aren't really important in the scheme of life. There are just things that I want to do while I travel the road of life. I need to devote more time in doing the things that are right, like quit all the fighting and walk by faith, not just sight.

I will show more love and not always the side of hate, because this world is winding down real fast and there's no time to waste. I want to see my name written down in the Book of Life, so I need to start today continuing doing what is right.

I know that Satan is very busy, and I'll be under attack, but I'll wear my spiritual shield of armor, which will even cover my back. Every day I will start with a prayer, and always focus on the good, as I reach out to others and live the life that I should.

So don't let this opportunity pass you by, when you get out of your bed, and have life make you cry. Don't just stretch and look around, keep these thoughts because they are sound. In your head remember what I told you; this world is winding down, and there aren't many choices. So start living your life righteously right now, because Jesus my friend is coming to town!

WOW!!!

What was I doing?

I was lying on my stomach with my panties on, twittering my thumbs with the TV on. I had it on mute while I talked on the phone; shucks I'm so lonely since you've been gone.

My day went so quickly while I was doing my thing. I was so happy that I started to sing. I wrote a book that was released today, now I'll sit and wait as I clock my pay. I want to get paid in a very fast way, but I will continue to dream until I'm rich one day!

So now that my day has come to an end, I'll start over tomorrow taking care of business from beginning to end. So when you call on me and wonder what I've been doing, I will still be busy with the things I'm pursuing.

Terry E. Lyle

What would it take to be Happy?

What would it take to be happy again? Just spending more time, with some of my friends? Maybe I'll chase away the blue skies of doubt, when from my mind I'll throw them out.

What would it take to be happy again? Should I prance around while I pretend? There's a battle going on in my head, sometimes frustrated, I wish I were dead.

What would it take to be happy again? Perhaps it would take a pint of ice cream and a bottle of gin? Trying to get drunk and chase away the blues, because being unhappy is now tattered old news.

What would it take to be happy again? It could be some comforting words from a dear old friend? Someone who would listen and be there for me, I'm sure it would be a moment that's happy for me.

Agendas

I was talking to a friend of mine today and we were discussing how people are always trying to use you, or they have an agenda. That gave me cause for thought. If everybody has an agenda, then I must have one as well. Agenda's don't always have to be negative in nature; it could be the agenda of solidifying a friendship, or it could be an agenda of not being alone. You could have an agenda of seeking knowledge from someone that you admire. Well true as well, some agenda's can be crucially damaging. It never seems to amaze me how ruthless and socially scumbag some people are. They blend in so well, while they lay in wait to pounce, because of their secret agenda. You offer the best part of yourself to others, yet they tear you down in their selfish, greedy, unrelenting manner, without thought or concern. Some people have an agenda of sucking you dry and draining you of all the innocence of sharing. So, the next time someone tells me that they don't have an agenda, I'll be leery, smile, and nod in agreement, as I walk away and think, "live long enough and you will."

Sugar Daddy

You come over here begging for my body, acting like you are expecting something, but you're not my sugar daddy so you will get nothing. You have the nerve to call me late at night, you must be crazy or you are looking for a fight.

While you're expecting to get somewhere, why don't you please get out of my face because I don't care? If you think you're going to get close to me, then you've wasted your time foolishly.

You know somebody must have told you wrong, so knucklehead you need to head on home. You never spend any money with your cheap behind. But you're running over here, spending gas and wasting my time.

I know my stuff is good and you must know it's true, so is that the reason you're in my face and acting like a fool? Your time has passed to step up your game, and your maneuvers towards me are totally lame.

So now when I hear your voice on the phone, I will tell you don't bother and please stay at home. Worry someone else and leave me alone. I'm so sick of your butt, and this should have been known.

Chaos

Awakened in the middle of the night by the sound of someone pounding against the window pane, heart racing as you jump up to investigate. "Oh no," you think, "not him again" while wondering why he will not leave you alone. Fear grips your heart and your stomach is tied into knots, as shakily you dial 911. The police finally arrive, illuminating the room with the blare of their bright light. This is the same old story once again, and you wonder will you ever feel safe. Sleepless nights are piling up and the toil begins to show on your face, as you try to keep your dark secret from the world outside. You're a victim of emotional and physical abuse. Afraid to share your fear and scared to fight back, as you feel like mush on the inside. Your self esteem has dropped to a new low as you protect the illusion that everything is fine. You continue smiling on the outside while your life is filled with chaos.

Children

Breathing deeply as I wonder in amazement, the depths of the mindset of a child. At what lengths would children go through in their quest to struggle forward towards adulthood? I've had the fortunate opportunity in my time to watch and monitor these young people. Yes, I've been the glorified babysitter for both family and friends. My instincts told me to treat them with respect and patience. Many times after witnessing their ungrateful manner, I wanted to treat them to a belt. I think some of them need to be on lock down and treated like raw recruits in boot camp. Taking away all frills and extras, while giving them nothing but food. Some children appear to think that they are entitled to do as they please without consequences. When did they go from precious to hateful and selfish? They are still tender in years. When did their mind turn inward towards lies and deceit? Why is their innocence cloaked in mischief and deceptions? Was the turning point society's fault? Was it negative media, or lack of supervision? I'm willing to accept my part on what difference I could have made. Today I will be a better role model and example because I too was a kid. Children don't consider the responsibility that comes with adulthood, where all provisions aren't provided for. There are predators out there waiting to devour. Our mission should be to teach young minds before it's too late. Unfortunately kids are dreamers, and some have detoured into fantasy land.

WOW!!!

I can't trust you

I thought that I could trust you, but I see that I can't. I was a fool to think the bond between us was as strong as I thought. How easy it appears for you to lie to my face as well as to me on the phone. I sit here disappointed and hurt, to finally realize that you are dishonest at the least. I openly communicated with you over the phone how I felt. Painfully I asked questions of you that were on my mind, in hopes for an honest answer. Fate intervened and exposed you for the liar that you really are. Somehow what you really felt accidentally got recorded, and I have proof in your own voice of who you really are. I'm hurt but I won't stoop to your level and try to justify the truth with your spin on it. Excuses I'm sure you have a few, along with the apologies that spew out of your mouth once you have been busted. Many times I felt an overwhelming desire to dismiss you from my life. I allowed myself to be sucked back in with the hopes of change. My heart quivers in my chest from the shock of the realization that I can't trust you. How hard it was for me to even believe you were worthy to share my inner most secrets. And when I decided to take a chance on you, then you lied to me. Save the explanations, if the truth isn't in you. What you sow you will reap. Think about how you will feel when you realize that the person you put your faith in will be the one you can't trust!

Terry E. Lyle

The Body Beautiful

Looking at different bodies can be very stimulating, their skin tone superb and muscle definition strong and ridged. Glancing around you will see some bodies that will make you salivate in wishful thinking. Some bodies excite you by the touch. The skin is like different flesh coats which we wear. Some appear more fashionable than the next. I find after awhile that looking at some bodies doesn't turn me on, it just leaves me empty. What I find sexy and appealing about the body are the similarities from the ones I've been intimately close to. How I can think about the softness of their touch, the curve of the dimples in their cheek, and the way they lay on their side, while rubbing their legs together slowly up and down. When I look at your body, I also touch your soul. We connect on a deeper level, where the physical appearance pales in comparison. When I watch you sleep and glance at your body in the fetal position; that to me is "The body beautiful".

Welcome

To

Appendix A

Appendix A

Here in my special corner is a special treat of works, submitted by my family and friends, from whom I have permission to include.

A-1   Mistakes, by Jaguar NL Lyle

(My handsome, first, and talented grandson)

A-2   Challenges, by Tracy D. Arnold

(My beautiful, compassionate friend)

A-3   Recovery, by Phillip Gardner Robertson

(My faithful and loving brother)

A-4   Life is so short, by Aleasa Basden

(A true blessing of friendship)

A-5   Don't judge me, by Alphonso Henderson

(A shining light in the darkness of the soul)

A-6   No Excuses, by Deborah Baldwin

(One of my oldest, dearest, living friends)

A-7   I just can't find the words, by Sylvia Robertson

(My awesome big sister, who's my anchor)

WOW!!!

Mistakes

By Jaguar NL Lyle

It is one thing to say I'm sorry for what I've done.

It's another thing to apologize for the mistakes we've made in the past.

But now, we've gone too far. We've lied, we've played, and we've even stolen from the ones who we knew had our back.

We all have made a mistake that we wish to God that we could take back.

Some have broken hearts; others have back stabbed, but us, we...

We have made the one mistake that is the most painful thing, and that is that we left each other over a thought that would never come true.

That one thing would be the thought of another person being with me, that isn't you.

I apologize for what I made you think, but I would never do you or any other like that, because I am a trustworthy person for you to be with.

Now do you see, was it, or wasn't it a mistake?

For the thought you had, it was a mistake.

Terry E. Lyle

Challenges

By Tracy D. Arnold

My heart grows weary of the same old behavior. I'd like to think of myself as a big girl, able to accept all challenges that life brings my way. Life has brought so many challenges my way such as the military, relationships, marriage, parenthood, college, the workforce, injuries, and now retirement. The children have grown into young adults. My spouse has chosen to work abroad and I've become oh so weary of all of the challenges that I singlehandedly have to handle. Now the challenge of sanity, happiness, and peace of mind in the midst of the hands with which I have been dealt are upon me. My closest companion can't be seen, but I can certainly feel his presence. My friends are few as people have shown that their primary agenda is to use and abuse me. The challenge of remembering who allows the challenges in the first place, the one who knows all, sees, all, and is all to everyone, is huge at this point. I pray that I can hold on while the ultimate challenges await me; the challenge to escape the trials, victoriously, yet to come; the challenge to overcome the tribulations that will come to try to cause me to stumble, and the challenge to stop the tears that never cease to be released. Those are the challenges that I look forward to overcoming. Then I will believe that this life has been worth living, because I am still in the race, I've haven't lost yet, and I'm a big girl now.

Recovery

By Phillip Robertson

Thank you, thank you, and thank you for my recovery, because of my God and what he's truly done for me.

Thank you, thank you, and thank you for my recovery, because God you have given my sister back to me.

Thank you, thank you, and thank you for my recovery, because of a new life I now can see all because God and my sister, never gave up, and had faith in me.

Thank you, thank you, and thank you, for my recovery, because of my sister's love that she has shown to me, while I was going through my most difficult and miserable recovery.

Thank you, thank you, and thank you for my recovery.

Life is short

By Aleasa Basden

Could have been me,

Should have been me,

Would have been me,

Had it not been for the grace of God!

Keep looking up that's where the blessings come from.

Don't Judge me

By Alphonso Henderson

Don't judge me because I don't fit your mold. Don't you know I'm carrying a heavy load?

Don't judge me because I'm not cool. I can't help it because I didn't finish school. Don't judge me because I am gay, I love who I am today

Don't judge me because I hate my brother, I don't need them I have a lover.

Don't judge me because I speak my mind, don't you think it's about time?

Don't judge me because I talk back to my mother, she left me alone with my two brothers.

Don't judge me because I don't look like you, I didn't have time to fix myself up; I had too much to do.

Don't judge me because I smoke crack. I did what I had to do that meant laying on my back.

Don't judge me because you have no right. I'll be with your husband in your bed tonight.

Don't judge me because I don't pray. Only God can judge me, he's doing it today.

Terry E. Lyle

No Excuses,

By Deborah Baldwin

Just fuss and fight, it just ain't right.

No it ain't cool, violence doesn't rule.

Keep it on the down low, "Oh gosh, bang, bang".
You don't know who had to go, just ain't no excuse for any kind of abuse.

Keep the Peace.

WOW!!!

131

I just can't find the words

By Sylvia Robertson

I just can't find the words to share
what's deep inside my heart.
It's filled with so much happiness,
I don't know where to start.
I heard a speech some years ago,
the words so clear, so wise.
I knew that very moment,
that one day we'd win the prize.
From Martin's lips we heard the dream,
one day we would be free.
To live a life of brotherhood,
God's plan, it was meant to be.
I watched him merge into the light,
of course there would be drama.
How dare he seek to change the world,
This man they call "Obama".
Armed with intelligence as his shield,
integrity as his sword,
It takes a whole village to raise a child,
this truth we can't ignore.

Terry E. Lyle

Children should not be left to choose
who they should look up to.
It's our job to be responsible.
That's what real parents do.
As I watched him take his lovely bride,
his family at his side,
into the halls of history,
all I could feel was pride.
The day they danced before the world,
it was so clear to me,
that love, respect, and family
was their first priority.
It takes more than experience
to solve the problems of today.

Compassion, good sense, and diligence
will help to pave the way.
Our future is based on family,
encompassing everyone.
Not only in America,
The world family must act as one.

We heard the dream of Martin.
We prayed to see the day.
And now that day has finally come.
Thank God, we're on our way.

WOW!!!